Beautiful
Cats & Kittens

Beautiful Cats & Kittens

The world's familiar breeds
and helpful hints on cat care

Edited by John Gilbert

Cathay Books

Contents

From Forest to Fireside

The cat is an enigmatic creature. It looks at you with that unblinking, steady gaze, conveying not the slightest hint of what is running through its mind. Try to insist on its doing something and the chances are it will do the very opposite. Accept it on its own terms and it will reward you with companionship, even close affection. For those who love cats this air of secrecy, the suggestion of complete self-reliance and the utter

Below The caffre or Egyptian cat is thought by many to be the ancestor of Short-haired domestic cats.
Right The ocelot, a small American wild cat, is easily tamed and is becoming increasingly popular as a pet.

lack of deference are precisely those features which make them so fascinating — far more interesting, for example, than dogs with their eager desire to curry favour and offer unquestioning obedience. Cat haters, on the other hand, retort that the animal's aloofness borders on contempt. They feel acutely uneasy in its presence. For them the cat is sly, ungrateful and not to be trusted.

Cynics might claim that throughout history man has behaved in a totally irrational manner towards the cat. When he has not been festooning it with garlands and worshipping its image in temples he has accused it of being in league with the devil and tossed it into the flames. What other household pet has had to witness such sudden shifts of opinion and endure such extreme reversals of fortune? Admittedly cat-headed deities and witch-burnings now belong to the distant past but have our attitudes really changed, what with championship trophies and medals at one end of the scale and horrifying incidents of negligence and cruelty at the other? No other animal has given rise to such a wealth of superstitious belief; and none has aroused such extremes of fervent devotion and bitter revulsion. It is often said that you either love or hate the cat, that there is no room for neutral feelings. Be that as it may, the cat seems unaffected. It goes its own way — aloof, proud and inscrutable.

Obscure origins

How fitting, then, that this aura of mystery should extend far back into time, shrouding the very origins of the domestic cat. Fossil remains of recognizable cats date back about ten million years but their wild ancestors are at least four times older than that. The trouble is that there is no clear line of evolutionary descent as exists in the case of the horse and (though disputed) the dog.

It is widely believed that the

Above left This scene from a Roman mosaic shows a cat attacking a cock.
Left Superstition in the Middle Ages. A 15th-century woodcut depicting a witch and her evil-looking black cat.
Right Dick Whittington and his cat — an early programme cover from London's Drury Lane Theatre.

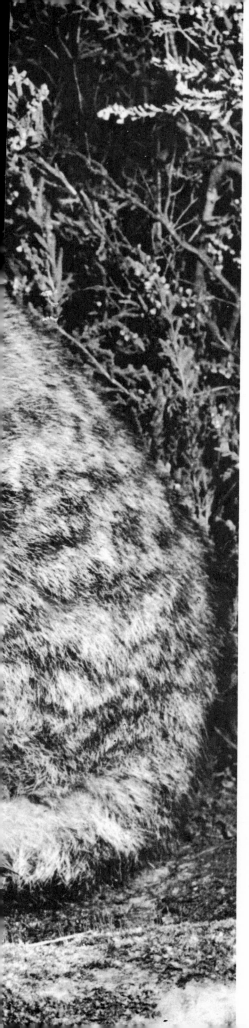

The wildcat, common in Britain
until the early 19th century, is still
occasionally seen in the Scottish
Highlands.

ancestor of the cat was a small carnivore called *Miacis* which more
resembled a weasel than a cat. Indeed, this creature, along with
related species of the family Mia-
cidae, may have been the common
ancestor of modern cats (Felidae),
dogs, (Canidae), bears (Ursidae),
civets (Viverridae), weasels (Mus-
telidae), raccoons (Procyonidae) and
hyaenas (Hyaenidae). Zoologists
consider civets and (despite their
dog-like appearance) hyaenas to be
closely related to the cat family.

Judging by fossils, primitive cats
possessed much larger canine teeth in
the upper jaw than do their present-
day counterparts. The tusks of the
sabre-toothed tiger protruded below
the chin even when the animal's
mouth was closed. Another sabre-
toothed cat, *Smilodon,* was probably
as large, though not as agile, as the
modern lion, with six-inch-long
canine teeth. But the sabre-toothed
cats were too large and heavy to
compete with more resourceful
hunters, their enormous teeth prov-
ing a handicap in the quest for food.
Eventually they became extinct.
Modern cats, both wild and
domestic, trace their descent (though
there are a number of missing links)
from another branch of the family,
whose members adapted more
successfully to changes of climate and
habitat. Today wild representatives
of the cat family are found not only in
forest, bush and savannah but also in
desert and mountain regions.

Tooth and claw

The cats of the family Felidae are
highly specialized carnivores with
powerful, streamlined bodies, keen
senses and well developed brains.
Despite its more peaceful temperament and seemingly indolent attitude, the ordinary household cat has
much in common with its jungle
relatives. It walks silently and
delicately on its softly padded toes.
Shedding its milk teeth at about six
months it develops a set of thirty
adult teeth, sixteen in the upper jaw,
fourteen in the lower. These are
typical of a carnivore, the two long,

sharp teeth in front being designed
for catching and killing prey, the
sharp-edged molars for paring meat
from the bone, the rest being non-
functional. There are no flat-
crowned teeth for chewing so that all
food has to be cut up into small pieces
for swallowing. The tip of the tongue
is covered with papillae, coarse rasp-
like bristles which help the animal to
strip meat from a bone, lap milk and
clean its fur. The long whiskers, con-
nected to nerves, are sensitive organs
of touch complementing keen vision
and acute hearing. The eyes are
large, usually rounded, the iris
equipped with a dilating muscle
which can respond suddenly to light
changes. In dim light the pupil is
widely exposed, allowing the max-
imum of light to pass through to the
retina. In bright light the opening
contracts into a vertical slit.

If the cat's sharp teeth are for-
midable weapons, so too are its
powerful claws. The combined ef-
ficiency of teeth and claws is of
course most dramatically in evidence
in the wild when tiger, leopard,
lioness, cheetah or jaguar pounce on
prey, and claws rip into the victim's
body, gripping tightly as fangs sink
into the throat to sever the vital
blood vessels. But the domestic cat
uses similar methods to immobilize
and destroy a mouse or a bird. In all
breeds, apart from Siamese, the
claws are retractile (capable of being
sheathed when not in use). This claw-
sheathing mechanism is a feature of
all wild cats too, with the exception
of the cheetah.

Family of hunters

Although there is still room for con-
troversy, experts have divided the
Felidae into five genera. The
cheetah, which superficially
resembles other large spotted cats
such as the leopard and the jaguar, is,
because of its rounded, only partially
retractile claws, classified in a separate genus *Acinonyx.* The claws
are more suitable for running over
hard ground and the cheetah is in fact
the fastest land animal in the world,
capable of a speed of 70 miles per
hour over a short distance. The
cheetah, incidentally, is one of the
few big cats to have been partly
domesticated. The Egyptians trained
the animal for hunting over 3,000

years ago. Later, in the Middle Ages, it was similarly used for coursing in India and the Near East, being hooded in the same manner as small birds of prey and gradually accustomed to obeying commands. It failed, however, to breed in captivity. Also occupying a separate place in the family is the clouded leopard (*Neofelis nebulosa*), whose upper canine teeth are longer than those of other cats.

The various species of lynx, including the northern and Canadian lynxes and the smaller North American lynx or bobcat, all belong to the genus *Lynx*. These animals are distinguished by a short tail and tufted ears; they also have only two premolar teeth in the upper jaw, as against three in other cats.

Slight variations in skull structure bring together the largest cats — lion, tiger, leopard, snow leopard and jaguar — all classified in the genus *Panthera*. Another distinctive feature is their voice, which is a roar, for they are incapable of purring in the manner of the remaining members of the cat family which are grouped together in the genus *Felis*.

So, according to this classification, the closest relatives of the domestic cat include the puma (or mountain lion), the serval and the caracal, as well as lesser known and smaller species such as the marbled cat, the margay, Geoffroy's cat, the jungle cat and the jaguarondi. The puma has a plain coat (although cubs have black spots) but most other species display irregular spots, blotches or stripes. Clearly there is a closer resemblance between the domestic cat and certain of these smaller wild species and it has been suggested, at

Above left *A female puma and her cub. The youngster's spots will fade as it matures, the adult coat being plain buff or reddish-brown.*
Left *The tiger, confined to Asia, is the largest of the cat family.*
Above right *The Gayer Anderson cat, an elegant bronze figure in the British Museum.*
Right *Detail of a bronze statue of the cat goddess Bast. In her right hand is a sistrum, an early musical instrument.*
Far right *A Peruvian gold puma mask with a design of double-headed serpents, from about the 6th century A.D.*

Far left Despite its placid appearance the African jungle cat is a fierce and relentless predator. Indentification features include lynx-like ear tufts.

Left A six-week-old bobcat or bay lynx. The fur of this North American member of the cat family will turn darker and the ear tufts become longer as it grows.

Below A lioness relaxes with her cub. Soon she will teach it how to stalk and kill prey. The lioness, with a typically low-slung muscular body, is essentially a hunter whereas the more massive, heavily built lion is the defender of territory and protector of the pride.

Right Now little larger than a domestic cat, this playful lion cub will be a full grown adult within three years.

various times, that either Pallas's cat, from central Asia, the Indian desert cat, the African bush cat, or the European wildcat may be the direct forerunner of the household cat.

Although attempts to domesticate these species have proved futile, one small wild cat which has been successfully tamed is the ocelot, an American species which adapts well to captivity and can make an intelligent and playful pet.

The relationship is established, yet the final links in the puzzle are missing. Apart from the absence of fossils from early populated sites, no cave drawings of domestic cats have been found and although classical mythology abounds with references to dogs, horses, bulls, birds, serpents and invented monsters, there is no mention of cats. The reason is that the cat, as time goes, is a relative newcomer to the company of man; and when he did accept her, entirely on her own terms, it was not for any utilitarian purpose. Her skill in hunting vermin was incidental, an added bonus. In fact the cat was a god before ever becoming a pet, a miniature version of the lion — long a royal and divine symbol of power. In those days the lion was more widely distributed than it is today, as familiar in western Asia and parts of Europe as it was in Africa. For many the lion was identified with the searing heat of the tropical sun. Hindu scriptures, for example, describe how the god Vishnu returned to earth for the fourth time as a lion.

The cat divine
Ancient Egypt was lion country and it was here, some 5,000 years ago, that the cat assumed divine status and later (around 1500 B.C.) entered the household. Frescoes, tomb paintings and bronzes reveal it as a short-haired, slender, comparatively long-legged creature, not unlike the modern Abyssinian cat in shape but with tabby markings. This animal may have been the wild species known as the caffre or Egyptian cat,

Above The leopard, ranging through the bush and forests of Africa and Asia, is, unlike the lion, a solitary hunter.
Left A baby jaguar rests in the cool grass. This handsome species is the largest of the New World cats.

which is still found in that part of the world. Because of the similarity many experts claim a direct line of descent and point to the caffre cat as the ancestor, if not of all domestic cats, at least of most Short-haired striped breeds. With its faintly striped yellowish coat, banded limbs and ringed, black-tipped tail, the caffre cat could well be the precursor of some Short-haired breeds, particularly as the animal is known to mate with domestic cats. But there is no conclusive proof of the theory.

In its divine guise the cat was associated both with the lion-headed goddess Sekhmet (sometimes called the Eye of Ra, the sun god) and with the goddess Bast or Pasht, who was traditionally represented with a cat's head. The remains of tens of thousands of embalmed and mummified cats and kittens have been recovered in the vicinity of the temple raised in the goddess's honour at Bubastis, a city in the Nile delta, now in ruins. Bast was evidently a much-loved household goddess and her image appears not only on large bronzes but also in the form of small amulets for personal wear. In addition figures of cats were fashioned from copper, faience and gold, often in the shape of ear-rings and necklaces.

When alive, the domestic cat was protected, adored and worshipped; when it died the entire household would go into mourning. Killing one of these sacred animals merited the death penalty. There is a story of one Roman soldier stationed in Egypt who accidentally caused the death of a cat and was practically lynched by a furious mob.

The Egyptian authorities did not permit the export of cats from their country but in due course cats made their way abroad (if necessary by being smuggled, northward into Europe and eastward to the Orient). There are references to cats in Sanskrit literature dating back 2,000 years, and certainly the cat was a familiar animal in China and Japan at this early date. As for Europe, although the cat was certainly introduced into Greece, it seems that the Greeks did not emulate the Egyptians in treating the animal with anything approaching the same measure of respect and devotion. There is not a mention of the cat in

Greek mythology and only on a couple of vases do we find a cat-like animal depicted. Aristophanes refers to a cat in one of his comedies but in the context this was probably a wild cat. The Greeks paid due homage to the mighty lion, which appears on Cretan seals and, more impressively, in carved form, as on the Lion Gate of the citadel at Mycenae; but they do not appear to have been interested in its smaller cousin.

The Romans, however, overlords of Egypt, carried home the native cult of Bast and clearly pampered their household cats, leaving the images of their pets to posterity in a number of charming wall paintings and mosaics. In the wake of Rome's invading armies cats insinuated themselves into every corner of Europe, including Britain. The remains of one domestic cat have been discovered in a villa at Lullingstone in Kent. Northern Europe was the haunt of the wildcat, a few of which still roam the highland forests; and although no direct descent can be substantiated there can be little doubt that wild and domestic strains mingled, which helps to explain the variety in size and colouring displayed by modern domestic breeds.

Ally of the devil
Initially the cat was welcomed as a loyal pet and ally. Farmers everywhere prized it, as the Egyptians had done, as a relentless enemy of vermin. In the tenth century the Prince of South Wales, Howel the Good, decreed by law that a newborn kitten should be valued at one penny, at double that sum before catching its first mouse, and at four pence thereafter. Furthermore, anyone killing or stealing a cat stood to be fined the equivalent of its worth, payable in wheat. The method of assessing the value was to hold the dead cat by the tail, its body touching the floor, and then to pour wheat over the carcase until the tip of the tail was covered. The seller of a female cat had to guarantee that she would not 'go a caterwauling every moon, that she devour not her kittens, that she have ears, eyes, teeth and nails, and being a good mouser'.

During the Middle Ages the fortunes of the domestic cat were violently and horribly reversed. A cult involving the participation of cats, originating in the Rhineland and linked with the worship of the pagan Norse goddess Freya (whose chariot was said to be drawn by two black cats) was denounced by the Church as heretical. The panic spread all over Europe. Any form of religious heresy was punishable by torture, often by execution. Again and again we find records of cases featuring cats, accused of being in the service of the devil or even posing as the devil himself. Any unfortunate person found harbouring a cat, especially a black cat, might be denounced as a witch, with dire consequences. It was equally convenient to blame any natural misfortune or disaster — a crop failure, an epidemic or a sudden death — on witches and their evil cat consorts.

Such beliefs were reinforced by the lingering memories of pagan practices. The people of the northern plains had long known the cat as the corn-spirit, preventing their children from damaging the harvest by frightening them with tails of the corn-cat. In some regions the last sheaf of corn was called the cat's tail, and before reaping commenced a cat would be ritually garlanded with flowers and ribbons. In Silesia the reaper cutting the last sheaf was named Tom-cat and given a pointed tail to wear; and in Picardy the gathering of the harvest was preceded by a cat sacrifice.

The madness lasted for centuries. The first witchcraft trials in Europe occurred in the thirteenth century; and at the last recorded trials in England and Scotland, in 1712 and 1722 respectively, cats were still being named as witches' familiars. Witch-hunting was condoned and encouraged by the Inquisition. In France, on the annual Festival of St Jean, cats were secured in sacks and ceremonially hurled into bonfires. Although the practice was prohibited by Louis XIII, it was reinstated by his son Louis XIV — and this in the enlightened seventeenth century! The mania even spread across the Atlantic to the colony of New England. Yet even at the height of this terrible idiocy double standards seem to have been observed. Kings, nobles, prelates and monks, consenting to the burning of witches and cats, continued to keep the useful little animals as pets and hunters of vermin.

The cat triumphant

Eventually man came to his senses. The persecution ended and the innocent cat returned to the fireside, its virtues extolled by eminent writers, its beauty captured by painters. Samuel Johnson was one of many distinguished figures in literature to enjoy the company of cats and his pet, Hodge, was famous among his large circle of friends. The nineteenth century was the real heyday of the cat, especially in France, where it was lauded in prose and verse by Baudelaire, Mallarmé, Taine, Gautier, Victor Hugo and many others. The steady stream of literature has since swelled into a torrent; and although there are some dissenting voices, the cat has been immortalized by such gifted writers as Lewis Carroll, Compton Mackenzie, Walter de la Mare, Colette, Carl van Vechten and T.S. Eliot.

Painters have also treated the cat with obvious affection but again it has only been during the last century or so that it has held the centre of the stage rather than being consigned to an obscure corner. The Japanese genius Hokusai painted cats in all shapes and moods. The work of the Swiss artist Gottfried Mind consists almost exclusively of drawings and paintings of his pet cats; and on a more popular level Louis Wain has delighted generations of cat-lovers with his witty caricatures. Cinema and television have recently provided the cat with new arenas of activity, both in leading and supporting roles; and in the field of animated cartoon only someone entirely lacking in humour could take issue with artists who find it more rewarding to depict the cat as a cunning, often somewhat obtuse, predator rather than a passive, compliant fireside pet.

The cat in art, seen here in the foreground of The Return of Ulysses *by the late 15th century painter Pinturicchio.*

A Family Affair

A pregnant cat, whether her mating has been deliberate or accidental, will require special care during the nine weeks or so preceding the birth of her litter. Experienced breeders can tell quite early on, simply by handling, whether a queen is pregnant, but it is almost always evident about three weeks after mating. First a slight reddening of the nipples will be seen, then she will steadily put on weight and inches. During the first month no additions to the standard diet will be necessary but later on amounts of protein, in the form of meat and fish, should be increased, with small doses of calcium lactate and olive oil. There is no need to stick inflexibly to rigid meal times as she may crave food at the oddest hours. But do not over-feed.

The gestation period of a female cat is between sixty-three and sixty-five days. In the ordinary way the mother will make her own preparations for the coming birth; and even if you try to lend a hand by offering her a box lined with newspaper the chances are that she will wander off and have her litter in

the airing cupboard or a wardrobe. On the other hand she may derive encouragement from your presence and even require your help should there be complications. So if you own a queen it is your responsibility to know what is going on. There are plenty of manuals on the subject and if you equip yourself with such simple aids as a small towel, some paper tissues and a hot water bottle, you will be prepared for all contingencies. But if you are doubtful of your ability to help in the event of things going wrong, have your vet at the other end of the telephone.

When her time is near the queen will probably settle down comfortably in her box or dark corner. As the second stage of labour begins her contractions will become stronger, usually occasioning nothing more than noisy purring, and in due course the first kitten will emerge, completely blind and enveloped in its sac. The mother will immediately rupture the umbilical cord and start licking the kitten vigorously, this action helping to stimulate circulation. Other kittens may follow quite quickly — there may eventually be as many as six or seven — but it is possible that up to two hours will elapse between each birth.

Assuming the births are normal and that you are not called upon to give assistance (even if a kitten appears tail first the queen will usually manage to expel it successfully) all

Left Three attractive Turkish Van kittens scramble over a log.
Below A simple newspaper-lined carton serves the needs of this mother and her mixed litter.

you need do is to change the bedding, make sure the family is warm, and that there is a saucer of water close to hand. Visit the scene at intervals, however, to satisfy yourself that the mother is eating and drinking properly and that the babies are suckling. Provided she has plenty of milk and the normal maternal instincts, the queen will happily take charge.

If there are too many kittens for her to cope with, remove them as soon as possible. Failing a friend who is willing to accommodate them, hand them over to your vet or to the nearest branch of one of the humane societies. If an alternative home cannot be found, the unwanted kittens will be painlessly put down. It is generally easier to find a home for a male and if the litter is mixed sexing is quite simple by comparing the kittens. A male has rudimentary testicles bunched half an inch or so from the anus; a female has a small slit, the entrance to the vagina, close to the anus.

The kittens which you do decide to keep will open their eyes at seven to ten days and will develop rapidly from this point. At about three weeks they will begin moving around, struggling out of their box and onto the floor. The mother will see to their toilet training and a sanitary box should be left close by. Soon they will be ready to be weaned and you will have to prepare supplementary meals, such as a mixture of evaporated milk, boiled water and glucose. Serve it on a saucer, dipping your finger into the milk and placing it on the kitten's lips. It will soon get used to the taste and be willing to lap it from a spoon or directly from the saucer. Once the kittens are lapping

Above left *The eyes of these young Abyssinian kittens are not yet open.*
Left *A large litter of one-month-old Siamese kittens, ready to abandon their basket and go exploring.*
Top right *White kitten cautiously confronts a stranger.*
Centre right *The Turkish Van cat, originally from the Lake Van region of Turkey, is a relatively new breed.*
Right *Three is a comfortable number for this White Persian mother to rear.*
Following pages *Family friends — Russian Blue kittens and Dachshund.*

freely, the amount of milky food should gradually be increased and solids introduced by stages — steamed fish, raw beef, chopped poultry and rabbit, baby cereals, raw and scrambled eggs, etc. At about eight weeks the kittens will be weaned and may be removed from the mother, by which time they are ready to fend for themselves.

Left *A pair of sprightly Black and White kittens.*
Below left *This fluffy kitten is no less adorable for being non-pedigree.*
Right *Easy transport at an early age. The mother holds her head upright so as not to bump her kitten on the ground.*
Below right *Mother's eyes are orange and those of her kittens, although blue at birth, will probably change within four to six weeks.*

Above These kittens are still barely able to stand but will be scampering about freely in a few weeks.
Left A lively family of Long-haired Cream and Orange kittens.
Right Maternal grooming for a Turkish Van kitten.
Following page left This fine Burmese cat has given birth to an attractively mixed litter.
Following page right Downtrodden — the smallest Siamese kitten competes for room on the cat walk.

You and Your Cat

The cat is an intelligent, independent, self-reliant creature. Thanks to native wit and stamina it is capable of withstanding hardship and of weathering crises far more successfully than most other domestic animals. But there are times, particularly during the early months, when it cannot look after itself. A kitten requires special attention and care if it is to grow into a healthy cat; and the adult cat must also be properly accommodated, fed and groomed if it is to remain in peak condition. So you, the prospective owner, should realize from the very outset that to share a home with a cat represents a certain measure of responsibility as well as giving a great deal of pleasure.

Below Vitamin-rich oils are useful to a cat's daily diet.
Right Three kittens in a family make an ideal number for they will grow up together as staunch friends.
Below right Two newly born kittens are kept warm with a hot water bottle placed under a blanket. This is a helpful temporary arrangement if the mother is having a difficult delivery.

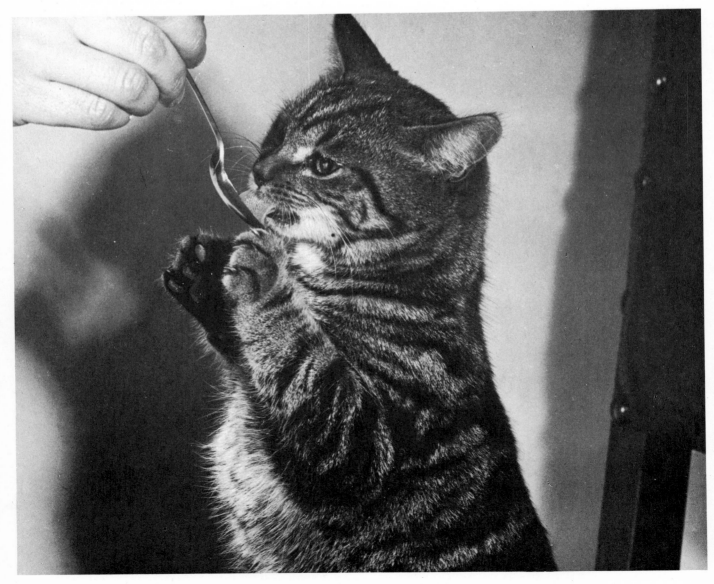

Left If, for any reason, a mother is
unable to suckle her newborn kittens
alternative feeding arrangements
must be made without delay. Since cow's
milk is unsuitable, a satisfactory
substitute for mother's milk has to be
prepared, such as unsweetened
evaporated milk, water and glucose.
This kitten is being fed through a
doll's bottle.
Right With breakable objects around,
a playful kitten needs supervision.
Far right The kitten in this basket is
well protected from draughts.
Below Three kittens contentedly lap
milk from a saucer.

Choosing a kitten

There are various ways of acquiring a kitten. Chance may take a hand, for example, in the shape of a stray or a gift from a neighbour or friend. Be careful before accepting such kittens into your home, no matter how appealing they look. Unexpected arrivals may prove to be health hazards and you should certainly consult a veterinarian before giving the newcomer house space, particularly if you already have other cats or domestic animals around.

Alternatively, having decided you would like a kitten as a pet, you may answer an advertisement in a local newspaper or fall in love with a kitten in a pet shop. In such circumstances the question of pedigree will not worry you and the kitten you get will probably be of mixed, partly unknown parentage. There is no reason why a non-pedigree kitten should not turn out to be as happy, healthy and robust as any pedigree kitten; but it is likely to be more of an unknown quantity than a guaranteed pedigree animal. All the more reason, therefore, why you should be wary of accepting the first kitten you happen to be offered. Never buy 'sight unseen'.

Ideally your kitten should be nine or ten weeks old, with a full set of teeth, fully weaned and already on a mixed diet. Even if you are not an expert you should be able to determine whether it is healthy. There are certain clues to look for. Make sure, for example, that it stands steadily on its feet, that its eyes are wide open and

Above left Early toilet training for a kitten is extremely important. In case of accidents do not scold the kitten but pick it up and place it gently but firmly on the litter tray.

Left Happy is the kitten which has free access to a garden. Grass is not only a place for hiding but also, when eaten, a natural medicine aiding the digestion.

Above right Cats and children seem to have a natural affinity, but a small child must be taught how to handle its pet. Teasing and rough treatment are not appreciated by any cat.

Right A kitten, given the chance, will sharpen its claws on anything to hand, including furniture and curtains. A pole covered with carpeting is one of several forms of scratching post.

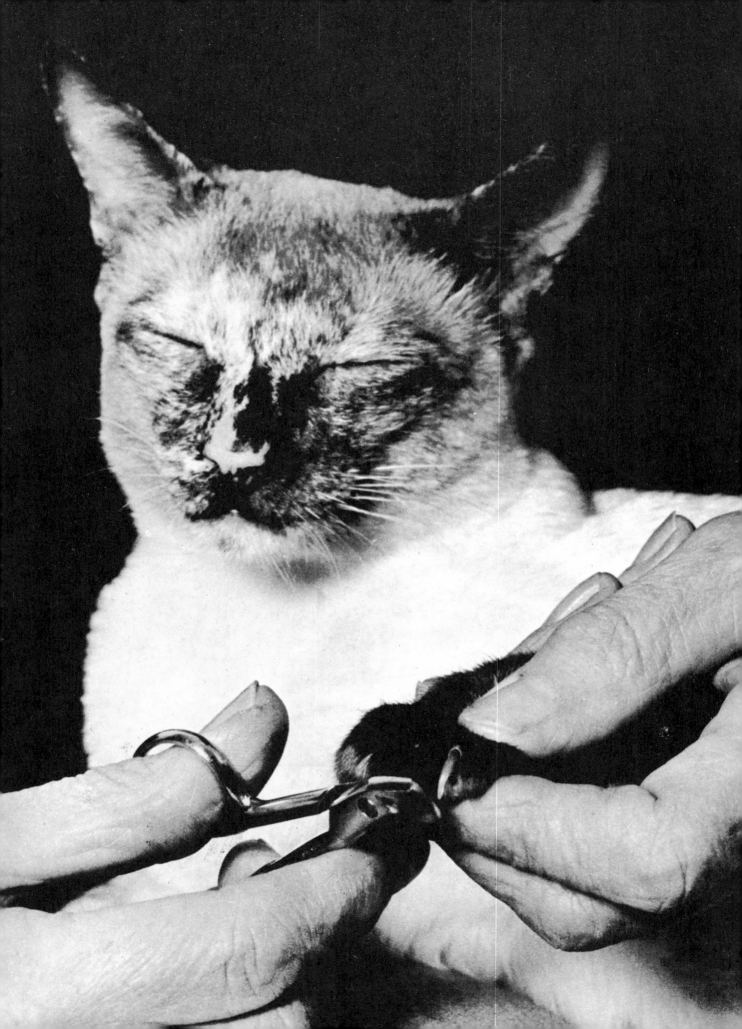

sparkling, that the inside of the mouth is a clear, rosy-pink colour and that the ears are clean, without any offensive smell or discharge. The nose should feel cool to the touch and not be running, there should be no signs of diarrhoea under the tail, the skin should be free of scabs and sores, and the coat should be soft and well groomed, without any black specks which may betray the presence of fleas.

These are a few obvious physical pointers to condition but it is also a good idea, if possible, to watch your kitten playing with other members of the same litter. At this age it should already be alert and lively, with a good sense of fun. If it appears to be unduly shy or nervous take a closer look at it before coming to a decision. Even a weak, timid kitten may grow up to be strong and assertive, provided it is basically healthy; but since all kittens are by nature gregarious it is possible that a kitten which persistently hides away in a corner may have something wrong with it. On the other hand, do not necessarily go for the obvious leader of the litter, usually easy to pick out as being the most active and vigorous member of the group. Such a pacemaker may well grow up into a hectoring, obstinate cat, not nearly so affectionate as its other, more reticent brothers or sisters.

If you have a mind to buy a pedigree kitten, however, with a view to breeding and showing, you will have to go to a reputable professional breeder who will surely give you every opportunity to observe the kitten in company and examine its condition. Obviously it will cost you more than a non-pedigree kitten but you will know exactly what you are buying. A good way of acquiring a kitten of a particular breed is to visit a cat show. If you cannot make a purchase on the spot you will certainly be put in touch with suitable breeders.

The breeder, whose reputation is at stake with every sale, should provide you with a copy of the kitten's pedigree, a form confirming

It is sometimes necessary to trim a cat's claws with special clippers. This Tortie Point Siamese seems to be dozing off during the operation.

that it has been inoculated against feline infectious enteritis, and full details of the diet it has been having. But whether your kitten is pedigree or non-pedigree, purchased from a breeder or from a shop, be sure to have it examined as soon as possible by a veterinarian who will make sure it is in good health, arrange for inoculation if not already done and give you invaluable advice on general care. Should he discover anything seriously wrong you must return it without delay to the point of purchase.

Welcoming the newcomer
Introducing a new kitten into your home requires tact and patience. After all, it has been abruptly removed from familiar surroundings, from the warmth and protection of its mother, from the company of its siblings. It is up to you to cushion the shock of entering a strange environment.

There is no need to go to a great deal of expense in preparing the new home for provided there is warmth and reasonable comfort the kitten will prove unfussy and adaptable. A simple cardboard box lined with a newspaper or blanket may be perfectly acceptable but you will probably prefer to accommodate the kitten in a simple basket with a blanket that can be changed frequently. Newspaper makes a very suitable under-covering. Make sure that the bed is placed in a warm place away from draughts. If the weather is exceptionally cold there is no harm in warming the basket with a hot water bottle. This should be placed under a blanket and on no account come into contact with the kitten's body.

The kitten will inevitably be rather shy and suspicious at first and should be allowed to find its feet in its own time. Try to situate its basket in a quiet place where it will not be exposed to sudden, unaccustomed noises — which includes the excited voices of children. Finding itself alone for the first time in its young life, it must be given every opportunity to get used to new faces and to explore its new surroundings without fuss and interference. It may not even accept food until it has overcome its initial mistrust and fear. This is nothing to worry about. A

bowl of slightly warmed milk left unobtrusively beside the basket may help win its confidence. Let it wander all over the place, exploring cupboards and furniture at will; but make sure that all windows are closed, that fireplaces are covered, that refrigerator doors are shut and that there is no way for the inquisitive little animal to find its way into washing machines and other domestic appliances. The kitchen conceals many potential death traps, and gas cookers, electric stoves and hot saucepans can cause terrible burns and scalds. Let it wander, by all means, but do keep a check on its comings and goings.

Cats enjoy the company of other animals and if you have to be out of the house during the day it is an excellent notion to buy two kittens which can keep each other company. But it is sometimes tricky bringing a new kitten into a home where there is already an established pet. An adult cat will take more readily to a new kitten than to another animal of its own size but the introduction must be done by stages. The principle is the same as for children with a new baby — a few days' isolation and then supervised contacts, with plenty of fuss being made of the established member of the family to show that there is no rejection or lack of affection. There may be much arching of the back, tail flourishing and spitting; but the chances are that there will eventually be full acceptance and friendship. Cats will also settle down quite happily with dogs and other household pets and here again acclimatization should be gradual so that there is no fear on the one side or jealousy on the other. But do not on any account leave the animals alone with one another until you are quite sure that they will not fight. The fact that cat and dog will establish amicable relations is proof that they are not natural enemies; but when the two do live together it is usually the cat which takes charge.

Small children have to be taught to treat the new kitten with loving care and gentleness. In their excitement they may be tempted to regard it simply as a novel kind of toy to be picked up, and pulled and tossed about at will. They must be told that a kitten needs plenty of sleep and should not be disturbed for a few days; and they should be taught the correct way of lifting it, supported with one hand under and around the back, the other under the chest, never picked up by the scruff of the neck.

Meals and titbits

A nine- or ten-week-old kitten requires four or five small meals a day, at regular intervals. If you have bought it from a breeder try to continue a similar diet and introduce new items very gradually. Remember that a kitten's stomach is only the size of a walnut and that it cannot cope with too much food at a time. No two kittens or cats will eat exactly the same type of food and it is impossible to go by set rules. Basically a cat needs proteins, carbohydrates, fats and minerals in different proportions, as well as vitamins to ensure normal growth and development. The more varied the diet the better.

At first a heaped tablespoonful of food for each meal will be quite enough. Two of the kitten's daily meals might consist of protein-rich fish or meat, the others of milk or milk-based foods, perhaps mixed with cereal or egg. Remember that milk alone is not sufficient liquid. Although some milk is important at this stage this will be the first of the meals to be refused and eventually dropped; and since cow's milk disagrees with many kittens, unsweetened evaporated milk is generally recommended. The same may apply even when the cat is fully grown and the saucer of milk may be disdainfully refused. Kitten and cat alike require plenty of fresh water and a bowl of water should always be available for 'between-meals' refreshment.

Meat and fish are staple solid foods and of the two meat is more important. Raw, lean minced beef is ideal and so is cooked, deboned chicken and rabbit. Fish should be given sparingly when the kitten is young and should invariably be cooked, with all bones carefully removed. In fact, fish need only be included for the sake of variety. On no account give your kitten an all-fish diet, for too much of it may cause a type of eczema.

Extra vitamins are always a good idea and can be administered, for example, in the form of halibut oil or cod-liver oil, mixed in with the milky meal. Grass, too, which also contains vitamins, is a natural emetic aiding the digestive functions. If you do not have a garden you can easily grow a variety such as cocksfoot indoors in a pot.

At twelve weeks or thereabouts you will be able to cut meals down to four a day and by the time the kitten is five or six months old it will probably be refusing its late afternoon meal and feeding only three times daily. When it has reached the age of nine months two daily meals, morning and evening, will be sufficient. These meals will, of course, become progressively larger and more varied, possibly including such meaty ingredients as cooked beef and poultry in addition to raw beef, cooked lamb and veal, raw and cooked liver (not too much raw as this may cause diarrhoea), raw or cooked kidneys, horsemeat (either raw or cooked but only if of a quality suitable for human consumption), a little raw or cooked heart, and cooked tongue. Cooked white fish, tinned pilchards, herrings, sardines and salmon, raw eggs, baby foods and cereals, and cooked vegetables also help to ring the changes. Busy people will find that proprietary cat foods are convenient to prepare and reputable brands are of course appetizing and nutritious. It is unwise to rely on such foods exclusively, however, and they should not be given to very young kittens because the contents are too rich.

Feeding is a particularly controversial topic and no two experts will be fully in agreement as to what to include and what to avoid. The cat, however, is an astonishingly adaptable animal and provided it receives the staple necessities of food and drink, the rest is largely a matter of temperament and taste. Foods which are generally considered unsuitable (fruit, nuts, cakes, ice-cream and the like) will usually prove innocuous, at least in minute quantities. Some cats enjoy gnawing meat bones but this is one area where special care is needed. Keep raw or cooked chicken and rabbit bones well out of reach from your prying cat for these may easily splinter, the sharp slivers

being capable of causing serious internal injury. As a rule, however, do not be afraid of indulging your cat now and then. Whether its preference is for sweets or savouries, the occasional titbit does no harm. But beware of going to the opposite extreme. Over-feeding can only cause your cat to become fat and lazy, perhaps ill.

Keeping clean

The cat is by nature a clean, fastidious animal but a new kitten has to be toilet trained. One most important piece of equipment, right from the start, is a litter tray. It must be low enough to allow the kitten to clamber in and out and should always be kept in the same place until the kitten becomes accustomed to using it regularly. You can either buy a plastic tray designed for the purpose or use a makeshift one in the shape of an oven tin. The tray may be filled in various ways — with sand, earth, ashes, peat moss or sawdust; or with a proprietary cat litter obtainable from pet shops. Whatever the contents, the tray must be emptied, cleaned and changed frequently. If a garden is within easy reach there will be no great problem at a later stage, but in confined surroundings such as a flat the litter tray should always be ready to hand.

Grooming is, of course, essential for any cat that is due to be put on show but it is just as important for a pet cat because dirty, tangled fur is not only unsightly but can easily harbour parasites and thus become a health risk. It is as well to get your kitten used to being groomed as soon as possible. The earlier it is accustomed to being handled the sooner it will look forward with pleasure to this routine. Washing is not essential. The natural licking process is quite enough for normal cleanliness and many cats, despite being intrigued by running or dripping taps, dislike any closer contact with water. A bath will only be necessary if your cat manages to get itself badly soiled, in which case use lukewarm water, be sparing of the soap (keeping it well away from the eyes) and dry

Even the best behaved kitten will get dirty from time to time and for wet paws a hair drier is quick and efficient.

thoroughly afterwards. Eyes and ears should, however, be regularly examined for dirt or signs of infection, and gently wiped, if need be, with slightly damp cotton wool.

In the case of certain breeds, including Siamese (whose claws are not retractile and grow very long), it may be necessary to clip the nails regularly, using special cat clippers. But the majority of cats which enjoy plenty of exercise and get outdoors keep their own claws in good condition by scratching on tree trunks and posts so that clipping is redundant. What they are doing is not so much sharpening the claws as exercising the muscles and removing the worn-out sheaths to expose the new claws underneath. Here again, however, some gentle but firm training may be required. Obviously you do not want your kitten to start shredding your carpets, curtains and furniture (which it may try to do if left to its own devices); so provide it with a scratching post. This can be bought in a pet shop or fashioned out of a rough log or piece of wood. When worn smooth it should be replaced with another.

It is the cat's fur, however, which requires the most regular attention; and naturally you will have to devote more time and care to Persians than to Short-haired breeds. The latter, if kept simply as pets, may need grooming only a couple of times a week. Use a fairly close-toothed steel comb to eliminate the odd flea and prevent hair getting matted, then brush thoroughly with a soft bristle brush. There is no harm in finishing off by wiping the fur with a handkerchief or chamois leather to give it a fine sheen. More frequent grooming may be necessary when the cat is moulting, as it normally will in spring and autumn. Whiskers are not shed at such times and the hair, of course, soon regrows.

Ailments and diseases
Grooming will help to keep your cat's fur in fine condition and reduce the possibility of it becoming infested

Cats and dogs are not natural enemies and will become the closest of friends as long as they are introduced to each other at an early age and suitable provision made for their individual needs.

by irritating parasites such as fleas and lice. Should this occur, despite your best efforts to prevent it, you should apply one of the recommended powders, but avoid those containing DDT. Examination of the ears is important in order to guard against ear canker, caused by mites. The first indication of this trouble may be when the kitten scratches its ears continuously or rubs its head repeatedly against the floor. Closer inspection may reveal the presence of a brownish fluid and this should be removed with dampened cotton wool around an orange stick. Your vet may also prescribe a canker powder or lotion to be applied regularly until the infection has disappeared.

Most cats suffer at one time or another from worms; and you should consult your vet in order to distinguish between round worms and tape worms so that the correct remedy can be applied. Round worms are very common in kittens and young cats and are easily treated with the appropriate pills. Care must be taken, however, in giving the tablets. The simplest method is to ask a friend to hold the kitten's forepaws and open its mouth wide while you cradle it in the crook of your arm and pop the pill in, releasing it at the back of the throat, then shutting the mouth and gently massaging the throat to make sure it has been swallowed.

The presence of tape worm may be suspected in a young adult cat which, although eating normally, appears to be thin and in poor shape. Since fleas are intermediary hosts the best way of avoiding tape worm is to keep a close lookout for fleas in the fur. Once the worm attacks the intestines it is difficult to eradicate and the advice of a vet must be sought.

An abscess caused by an accident or a fight with another cat may not immediately be noticeable but will soon be revealed as a hard, shiny, pus-filled swelling which grows steadily larger. Again professional advice should be taken since lancing or injection may be necessary. A bite, however, provided it shows no sign of turning septic, can be treated at home by bathing with a mild disinfectant. If, as a result of a blow or fall, you suspect a broken bone, keep the cat warm and call the vet at once.

Other common ailments such as diarrhoea and constipation may be due to an incorrect or altered diet. In kittens diarrhoea is often the result of too much milk being given and can be corrected by adding a little kaolin powder to the food. In adult cats, however, food should be withheld and only water given. Should the condition persist for more than a day, consult your vet. Constipation, which is normally avoidable if grass is included in the diet, can be eased with a teaspoonful of corn oil or mineral oil, but again, should it persist, take the cat to the vet in case there is a blockage caused by a furball or some other object.

Teething does not normally cause undue trouble. When at the age of five or six months the milk teeth fall out, to be replaced by the second set, a kitten may go off its food because of inflamed gums. A daily dose of milk of magnesia and finely chopped food should be given. An older cat may suffer from pyorrhoea, a disease caused when deposits of tartar build up on the teeth, pushing the gums back and exposing the roots. If not treated the sockets may become infected, leading to inflammation and loosening of the teeth, and this in turn to digestive troubles. Slip in hard dry foods (such as biscuits) in your cat's daily diet or give it a raw bone to chew and teeth ailments will probably not occur.

Colds may be caused by draughts, the symptoms being running eyes and sneezing. Given warmth and proper nursing, recovery should be rapid but if the symptoms persist consult the vet in case the trouble is more serious. Inflammation of the eyes, for example, may turn out to be conjunctivitis, a very contagious condition which demands immediate treatment.

There is every chance that your cat will go through life without contracting these or similar ailments; but if it does the attention of a good veterinarian will usually ensure quick recovery. There are, however, two diseases that affect kittens and cats which may be dangerous, even fatal. Feline infectious enteritis or panleukopenia is a viral disease which may kill in a matter of hours and which proves fatal in more than three-quarters of recorded cases.

Symptoms of the disease are generally a high fever, loss of appetite, slight vomiting and unusual lassitude. The kitten may sit crouched over its water bowl, either not drinking at all or taking only an occasional sip; or it may cower in a corner, taking no interest in anything. Immediate treatment is the only hope, and fortunately there are today a number of effective vaccines. If, when you first acquire it, your kitten has not already been inoculated against feline infectious enteritis, make sure this is done without fail, preferably between the ages of seven and ten weeks. If your cat dies of this disease you will have to take the most stringent precautions, burning its basket, bedding and toys, and thoroughly disinfecting the whole house. Nor should you bring another kitten into the home (and then only after it has been inoculated) for at least six months.

The other dangerous disease is pneumonitis, otherwise known as feline distemper or cat flu. This is a respiratory infection and the symptoms include running of the eyes and nose, coughing, sneezing, possibly diarrhoea, high fever and refusal of food. Careful nursing and a controlled diet usually bring about a complete cure but since it is a highly infectious illness the invalid must be kept away from other cats. Unfortunately the disease occurs in so many different forms that it has not yet been possible to devise a completely reliable antidote, although some vets do recommend vaccination. It is possible too that the feline infectious enteritis inoculation confers a degree of immunity.

Above left *Grooming is essential for all cats. With Short-haired breeds, especially for showing, a glossy sheen to the coat can be given by applying a final polish with a soft cloth, leather or silk handerchief.*
Left *A sprinkling of powder or bran is sometimes a valuable part of the grooming procedure, but all traces should be thoroughly brushed out afterwards.*
Right *A cat living in the country may collect burrs or even parasites in its coat. The former should be removed by hand, the latter eliminated by combing and vigorous brushing.*

Left An ordinary log for scratching will help to keep a cat's claws in good condition. When worn smooth it should promptly be replaced.

Below Although outnumbered, this kitten will probably grow up to be the dominant member of the trio.

Right A cat door, swinging on hinges, can conveniently be fitted to one of the outside doors of a house, affording easy entrance and exit at any time.

Left A cat does not need expensive and elaborate accommodation. This one seems quite happy in a cardboard container.
Above Siamese cats do not demand a special diet. As with all breeds, the important thing is to test a cat's individual likes and dislikes and make sure that its meals are well balanced.
Right A cat is quite capable of keeping its paws and other accessible parts of the body clean, but its own efforts must be supplemented by combing and brushing.

Walking Alone

The cat is an independent, self-willed and notoriously disobedient creature whose essential nature is admirably summed up in Rudyard Kipling's story *The Cat that Walked by Himself*. No question here of man striking the sort of bargain he did with the dog and the horse — food and lodging in return for work. The disdainful cat ('I am not a friend and I am not a servant') was inveigled by the woman ('wife of my enemy') who promised that if ever she spoke three words in the animal's praise it would be allowed to come into the cave, sit by the fire and lap milk three times a day. The cat obviously got the best of the bargain.

Punishing a cat for a misdemeanour is futile and self-defeating. In common with other animals it has no moral sense, as humans understand the term, and cannot distinguish between right and wrong. If it does something it is simply because it believes it will be to its immediate advantage, and vice-versa. A kitten can be toilet trained with a firm rebuke and a tap across the nose or rump; and once having learned this lesson there will be no backsliding. But it will take more than an angry lecture to stop a cat filching a piece of meat or even a cream cake if you are careless enough to leave such morsels within reach (and given its agility a high shelf in the larder is well within range). Even more fruitless, no matter how distasteful you may find it, is any attempt to curb a cat's natural hunting instinct.

Through the centuries the cat has been prized for its hunting skill. Three thousand years ago, in China and Japan, cats were employed to protect the silkworm cocoons from ravage by rats; in Egypt they killed snakes as well Today they still perform a valuable service on farms and in warehouses by keeping down the rodent population. But how should the cat know, as it stalks through the long grass on a bright spring day, that a fledgling is forbidden game?

In common with all the members of its family the domestic cat is instinctively a hunter. In the wild the leopard and cheetah kill simply to eat, their survival depending on their prowess. If, as a result of illness, injury or advanced age, they are unable to hunt, they starve. The cat has the best of both worlds. It is not compelled to kill in order to stay alive. Indeed even the best mouser has to be provided with its daily ration of food and drink. But the hunting instinct is still there. Watch your Tabby or Abyssinian stalking a bird. First it crouches, body tense, limbs flexed, fur bristling, ears pricked, eyes unwavering; then it moves forward, slowly and silently on padded feet; finally it pounces, claws unsheathed, eager for the kill. The chances are it will miss, but there can be no mistaking its origins!

Most big cats are nocturnal hunters and although domesticity has tended to reverse the pattern, many pet cats still go out hunting by night. A cat's vision and hearing are exceptionally keen but unlike most mammals it relies more on its eyes than its ears. The angle of vision is over 200°; the pupils can open very wide or narrow to a tiny slit (adjusting to a wide range of light conditions); and the eyes focus very rapidly. The reflecting layer behind the retina which makes it possible to increase the amount of light reaching the eye when it is dark is known as the tapetum; and it is the tapetum which causes the animal's eyes to shine at night when a bright light is directed at them. Although it actually cannot see in the dark, a cat can see much better than most mammals in a dim light. But the probability is that the cat is colour blind, living in a world where all objects are viewed in shades of grey.

The whiskers are extremely sensitive too, responding not only to

Acknowledging no debt to man, the cat, even though domesticated, remains independent and free.

direct contact but also to changes in air pressure caused by the nearby presence or movement of objects. The whiskers protect the eyes and, as secondary organs of touch, are a valuable asset in poor light.

Smell plays a lesser role in the hunting forays of the domestic cat (although a major part in its sex life), for it will be used only at short distances for precise location. Hearing is remarkably acute, perhaps even

Left *A Blue Point warily stalks its prey. Like other Short-haired breeds, Siamese are accomplished hunters.*
Below *Curiosity and a sense of adventure — hallmarks of any healthy kitten.*
Right *Only a Tabby kitten, but the lines of the body and the crouched posture hint at ancestral hunting blood.*
Below right *Study in concentration.*

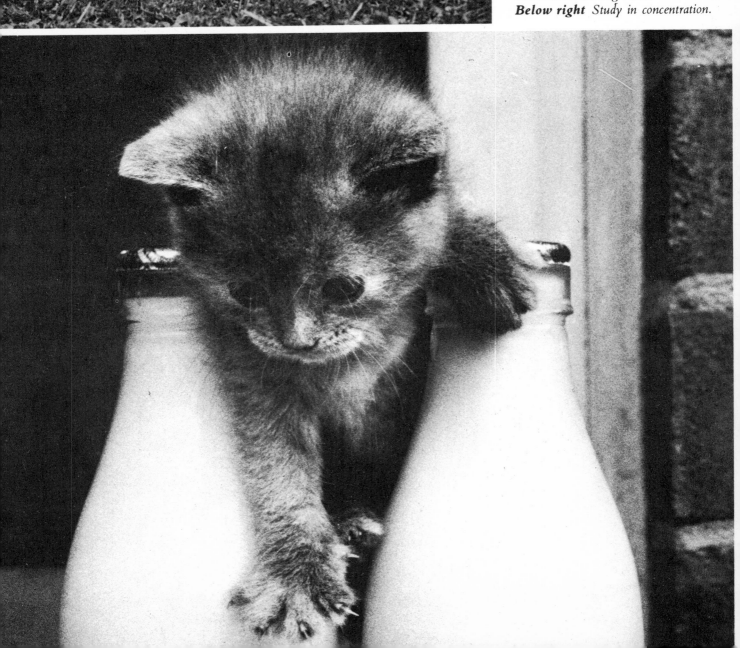

better than that of a dog. Each ear contains twenty-seven muscles which enable the visible part of the ear, the pinna, to be turned in several directions, picking up sounds far beyond the range of human hearing. Every owner has a favourite story of a cat which has suddenly sat up, pricking its ears and twitching its nostrils for no apparent reason. This type of sensitivity tends to encourage the belief that the cat is endowed with a 'sixth sense'. Even allowing for this, however, there are verified incidents of this nature which simply defy rational explanation.

Left *On the brink.*
Below left *Fur and fir.*
Right *Unwinking gaze.*
Below *So near and yet ...*

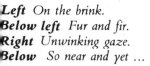

Short-haired Cats

Of the millions of cats living in all parts of the world, the vast majority are of the type generally described as Short-haired. Of these only a relatively small proportion are pedigree cats, conforming to the rigid standards laid down by the various Cat Fanciers' Associations. Call them what you will — non-pedigree cats, alley cats or mongrels — most of the cats that are kept in the home as pets or allowed to wander

Below The Tabby is the commonest and most popular of Short-haired breeds. *Right* There are literally millions of mongrel or non-pedigree cats all over the world. A pedigree Tabby should have no white marks anywhere.

aimlessly about the city streets, are animals of mixed parentage, the result of free mating over the years.

All that these non-pedigree cats have in common is their solid, sturdy build. Some are uniform in colour but in most cases the coat tends to be an arbitrary mixture of white and one or more other colours — black, brown, grey and ginger. A large number of them show tabby markings, also with random patches of white. It is a good thing that these non-pedigree cats are, as a rule, well loved and cared for; otherwise the number of homeless animals would be far greater. As it is, there are quite enough stray cats, without a proper home, to cause the various protection societies considerable concern.

Waifs and strays

In countries where cats are widely kept as pets there are a number of animal clubs and societies, some of them specializing only in cats, whose mission it is to educate the public in caring for their household animals and to provide special services related to their welfare. In Britain such societies, including the Royal Society for the Prevention of Cruelty to Animals, the Blue Cross Society, and the People's Dispensary for Sick Animals, are primarily concerned with cases of cruelty and neglect. They provide expert advice and, where necessary, treatment; and they have been instrumental in persuading the government to pass laws protecting animals from cruelty and unnecessary suffering. These societies work closely with branches and similar organizations in other parts of the world, including the Commonwealth and the United States. The American organization known as Pet Pride is probably the largest, non-profit-making cat club in the world.

Many cats become strays by accident, perhaps when their owners

Above left Genetically, white is dominant over other colours. The large areas of white on this cat's coat testify to its mixed parentage.
Left A household pet such as this, with its attractive and individual marking, could still win a prize at a show.
Right A delightful pair of non-pedigree Tabby kittens.

Left Black and white cats are common but for show purposes the two colours must be in exactly the correct proportions and on certain parts of the body.
Below This frisky ginger kitten could be registered for a show under 'Any other variety' but it is not an officially registered breed.
Right A Short-haired Tortoiseshell cat. Its coat contains black, dark red and cream, each colour being separate.
Below right The Short-haired Blue-Cream is a difficult cat to breed true. It is the offspring of Blue and Cream parents.

move house or go on holiday. This is a callous and deplorable way of treating a cat and can easily be prevented by making suitable boarding arrangements. Others are the progeny of parents who are already homeless. Such strays are known as feral cats, tough in body and character, with two principal aims in life — to feed themselves and to procreate. Suspicious by nature, they tend to shy away from human contact as much as possible. There are large feral cat populations in many parts of the world, as, for example, in Rome and Florence. These animals are often large and aggressive, defending their territories fiercely against all intruders, and should be approached with extreme caution.

A wandering cat that happens to turn up on your doorstep should not be fed until you are quite certain that it is a true stray. Even then you should not take it straight into the house but feed it somewhere outside. This is a sensible precaution, for the life of a stray is hard; and being prey to diseases there is every chance that it will be carrying parasites in its coat. It could thus be a health threat to your own pet should the two come into contact. If the stranger looks so pathetic or appealing that you feel bound to invite it indoors and keep it on as a permanent resident, you would be well advised to take it first to your vet for a clean bill of health. Once suitably treated for fleas and other parasites, it may well turn out to be as good a pet as any that you have found through other channels. A cat without a pedigree, whatever its origin, is potentially as affectionate, intelligent and companionable as one with a long and respectable family tree.

This problem of excess numbers is, nevertheless, a disturbing one. A mother who obviously cannot cope with all her kittens must not be left to manage as best she can; nor is it fair to give house space to a greater number of kittens than you are prepared to accommodate and feed. Having a kitten put to sleep is always a conscience-searing business but often a matter of common humanity. Do not be ruled by sentiment on such occasions; and once having made the decision have it done properly by a professional rather than try to dis-

pose of it yourself (for example, by drowning). In this way you at least have the assurance that no physical suffering will be involved.

Population control

The old saying 'prevention is better than cure' is especially applicable in this context. It is worth remembering that a healthy female cat is capable of bearing up to three litters a year and that each litter may comprise between four and eight kittens. The chances are that at least half of these kittens will be female, each of them being physically capable of procreating within the first year — from about five months onwards. Obviously, therefore, some form of birth control is essential if the cat population is not to get completely out of hand. So far science has not come up with a contraceptive pill for cats (although research is under way), so that the only effective answer at the present time is to have your pet neutered.

A kitten that is kept purely as a pet and not specifically for breeding purposes ought certainly to be neutered as soon as this is practicable. In Britain some authorities recommend castrating a male at about three months and spaying a female at approximately four and a half months, depending on development. Many people, however, prefer to wait a little longer, until a kitten is five or six months old, for if a male is neutered too early this may lead to bladder trouble in later life. In America some experts suggest waiting until the tom is eight months old and advise against spaying a female until after the first heat. It is quite possible, in fact, for the operation to be performed after she has given birth to her first litter.

A male kitten may be as affectionate as a female but when he becomes sexually mature he will follow his natural instincts and that is when trouble starts. Probably he will go roving the neighbourhood in search of a mate, often returning home battle-scarred and half-starving. Inside the house he will make his presence only too evident by spraying the carpets, curtains and

Although not the product of selective breeding, this farm kitten clearly lacks neither spirit nor charm.

furniture, leaving his pungent, unpleasant odour in every corner. The operation, which consists of removing the testicles, is simple and painless. In fact, provided your vet agrees, it is sometimes convenient for it to be done at the same time as the inoculation against feline infectious enteritis. It is simply a matter of leaving out the kitten's morning meal, taking him to the surgery in a basket and collecting him later in the day. He will be given an anaesthetic (as required by law) before the operation is performed and will be no worse for wear afterwards. Having taken him home, just wrap him up warmly and allow him to sleep as long as he wants.

Spaying a female kitten involves removal of the ovaries and uterus and is a little more complicated and time-consuming, possibly entailing an overnight stay in the surgery. When she returns home the only sign of the operation will be a tiny incision sewn with a few stitches. Although the kitten will perhaps refuse to eat or play in the customary fashion she will be herself again within forty-eight hours or so, and a week later she should be taken back to the vet to have her stitches removed. This too is quite painless.

In neither sex does neutering have the slightest adverse effect on a cat's physical development or character. It is true that a male whose basic urge to mate has been curtailed will be less prone to prowl about and will become more house-bound. All the more important, therefore, that such a cat should be encouraged to take plenty of exercise and that its diet should be very closely supervised. Obesity is the direct consequence of over-feeding and there is no reason for a neutered cat to become fat and lethargic. For affection and intelligence there is nothing to choose (and indeed it is hard to distinguish) between a neutered and an 'entire' cat. Incidentally, neutered cats can win prizes too for they may be entered for shows, competing against one another in classes of their own.

Heredity

A kitten's sex, coat colour, markings, eye colour and other physical characteristics are all determined by the genetic make-up of its parents.

Ultra-microscopic units of inherited material are thus passed on — as in all animal species — from generation to generation. When two pedigree cats of the same breed are mated it can be reasonably predicted that the kittens born to the female will inherit most of the dominant features of the parents. But there is a chance that a minority of such kittens will lack some of these features and be 'throwbacks', with recessive genes coming to the fore. Occasionally, too, irregularities may arise, possibly as a result of a dominant gene behaving in an unusual way.

These mutant genes can, in extreme cases, create entirely new breeds; at other times mutation will give rise to abnormalities. Some White cats, whether Short-haired or Long-haired, have a tendency to deafness. This is undoubtedly a hereditary trait which may recur after several generations in spite of the best efforts of breeders to eliminate the fault. Another fairly rare mutation may give rise to the condition known as 'polydactylism'. A normal cat has five toes on each front foot and four on each hind foot; but a polydactyl cat will have extra toes, either on the back or front feet. President Theodore Roosevelt's pet cat 'Slippers' had six toes on each foot.

In matings between two cats of different breeds the dominant genes will again influence colour and other physical features, but the results are more haphazard and unpredictable. Matings, for example, between Black and Tabby cats strongly indicate that the gene for tabby markings is dominant over black. Understanding how heredity works is all-important, of course, for breeders.

Genetically speaking, white is dominant over all other colours. A white mother will pass on her colouring to about half her kittens. This explains why so many stray or working cats have large patches of white on the coat, signifying their mixed ancestry. It is interesting to note, however, that this genetic peculiarity does not hold true for many other small animals. If it did all such animals in the wild would carry prominent white marking and this would completely destroy their natural camouflage.

The popular Tabby

The majority of cats, whether pedigree or non-pedigree, have short hair. The pedigree breeds which are recognized for show purposes vary to some extent according to the country concerned. In the United Kingdom the Short-haired breeds are divided into two principal categories, belonging either to the British or the Foreign type. Elsewhere the term Domestic is applied to the cats of the former group. The distinction is, in any event, somewhat misleading, for although the so-called Foreign cats originally came from abroad (most of them from the Far East) nowadays the best pedigree animals are bred at home.

In both types of cat the hair is short, stiff and compact, but obviously there are variations in colour and marking. There is also a notable difference in the shape of the body. The British cat has a slim, sturdy body (the term 'cobby' is often applied, signifying a low-lying body on proportionately short legs). The head is broad and rounded, with fairly short ears, a short nose and round eyes. The legs are of moderate length, the feet round, the tail short and thick at the base. The Foreign Short-haired cat, on the other hand, has a rather longer, lither body, a wedge-shaped head, tall ears and slightly slanting eyes. The legs too are longer, the feet small and dainty, the tail long and tapering.

The British Short-haired cat usually has a placid temperament, is ideal with children and does not seem to mind being picked up and handled. It is affectionate and intelligent and the only pity is that there are so few pedigree specimens being bred in comparison with other breeds.

The Short-haired Tabby, belonging to the British category, is probably the best known of all cats. What is more, it is regarded as one of the world's earliest breeds, as is suggested by Egyptian paintings which depict pet cats with tabby markings. The word 'tabby' appears to have been derived from Attabiah, a district in the old city of Baghdad, where a certain kind of beautiful water-marked silk was manufactured. The stripes and whorls on the cat's coat reminded one buyer of the pattern on the material and the name was apparently transferred to the animal.

Another delightful legend relating to the origin of the Tabby concerns the prophet Mahomet who is said to have caressed the cat and left the imprint of his fingers on the animal's shoulders (in markings that somewhat resemble the wings of butterflies) and on its forehead (where the dark lines that run down from the head and turn inwards towards the nose and top of the eyes often take on the rough form of a letter 'M'). The prophet's reputed fondness for cats is also recorded in a story which describes how he cut off the sleeve of his gown rather than disturb the favourite cat which happened to be lying asleep inside it.

There are two basic types of tabby marking, striped and blotched, and they are never both found on the same cat. In both types there is a ground colour over which lines of a deeper colour are superimposed, forming a distinctive pattern of lines, spots or small patches; head and cheeks are delicately pencilled in black; legs and tail are ringed. In the striped Tabby the bars and streaks across the shoulders look like butterfly wings when viewed from above; and in the blotched Tabby the longitudinal stripes form a horseshoe or circular pattern with clear circles, or chains, running around the throat and chest. In kittens the typical tabby markings are not always evident at birth but soon make their appearance; and it is interesting to note that in some other breeds the kittens show faint tabby markings at birth (which vanish later), suggesting that there must be some tabby blood in their veins. Incidentally, when a striped Tabby is mated with a blotched Tabby the striped pattern turns out to be dominant.

Most of the Tabbies that are normally kept as pets would fail to qualify for showing (except in the special classes reserved for household pets). The reason is that it is extreme-

Above right A contented British Blue queen with her newborn kittens.
Right Elegant stripes and rings adorn the body and tail of this sleek, relaxed farmyard cat.

ly difficult to breed a Tabby with the coat markings which conform exactly to the rigid standards laid down by the Governing Council of the Cat Fancy. Basically, for exhibition purposes, the markings have to be dense and quite distinct from the ground colour; nor must there be the faintest touch of white anywhere. In most Tabbies there tends to be some blurring of colours and the odd white patch.

Of the three Short-haired Tabby breeds recognized in Britain it is the Brown Tabby which most closely resembles the majority of household pets; but it is no easy matter to breed a cat with the necessary unsmudged, dense black markings and no vestige of white on chin and lips. The most popular breed is the Silver Tabby, again with distinct black markings and no break in the bands running down the back. The rings on tail and legs must be evenly distributed and the ground colour should be pure silver. Even if such standards are difficult to attain, a Short-haired Silver Tabby makes a wonderful pet, being extremely affectionate, fond of human company and very undemanding.

Particularly handsome, but even more difficult to breed true, is the Short-haired Red Tabby, a real aristocrat compared with the ordinary non-pedigree ginger cats that are so plentiful. The markings on this breed should conform to the general pattern for all Tabbies but they are a deep mahogany red on a rich red ground. The eyes must be hazel or orange, and white hairs or a white tip to the tail are regarded as faults. The difficulty in breeding stems from the fact that both the markings and the ground of the Red Tabby are variants of the same colour.

Sometimes exhibited in shows under 'Any other variety' is the Mackerel Tabby, which has fine vertical stripes instead of the conventional target pattern. The rings are narrow and numerous, running from the spine downwards. Any colouring is permissible.

Even if this Short-haired White cat happens to have green eyes and a scattering of darker hairs which spoil its show chances, it will still make an attractive and affectionate pet.

In the United States the Blue Tabby is a recognized breed. The ground colour of the Short-haired variety is pale blue with tan overtones and the markings are a dense dark blue.

Self or single-colour cats

If it is difficult enough to breed a show-worthy Tabby, the challenge of producing a pedigree 'self' or single-coloured Short-haired cat is equally demanding. The Short-haired Black cat is, of course, a popular household pet. Although no longer regarded as a familiar of witches, the ordinary Black cat is still the object of a wide range of superstitious beliefs. Curiously, whereas in Britain a Black cat is generally considered a lucky omen, in America it is regarded as unlucky. But such beliefs surmount national boundaries and vary from individual to individual, defying rational analysis.

In young kittens a tabby pattern is clearly visible before the coat darkens, indicating that a Black cat is really a Tabby, with the tabby pattern overlaid on a black ground. In this, as in other breeds, the tabby gene is dominant.

Many of the Short-haired Black cats kept as pets have green eyes, and this automatically rules them out for show purposes, since the standards stipulate deep copper or orange eyes, with no trace of green. Furthermore, there is quite likely to be some white mixed with the black, and this again is unacceptable for the prize specimen is expected to possess a jet black coat with no tinge of rust and no white hairs anywhere. This deep black colour is not easy to produce or maintain; and since wet grass can turn the coat rusty and too much sun bleach the hairs, the would-be champion is often obliged to spend a good deal of time indoors.

A pure White cat is even rarer than a pure Black. Show standards require the coat of this breed to be untinged with yellow and for the eyes to be a deep sapphire blue or, alternatively, orange. In the first place, the blue eye colour is difficult to acquire; secondly, a Blue-eyed White cat usually grows up to be hard of hearing, and this is naturally a deterrent to the breeder. The curious

Left The fur of this Short-haired
kitten will have to be combed and brushed
regularly to get rid of dirt and parasites.
Right The drawback to breeding Blue-
eyed White cats is that they are usually
hard of hearing.
Far right Short-haired Tortoiseshell
and White — a fairly rare breed.
Below The Short-haired Cream is
an infrequent competitor at shows. The
coat must ideally be clear in colour.
Even this kitten may later develop bars
on the legs and rings on the tail which
will disqualify it.

Far left A Russian Blue kitten.
Left The British Blue is regarded by some as the aristocrat of British Short-haired breeds.
Below The Orange kitten on the left is a male, the Tortoiseshell and White a female. Orange is the geneticists' term for a coat blending red, yellow and marmalade. In a Tortoiseshell cat the colours are in distinct patches. The orange influence is only completely dominant in the male; in the female the rest of the coat consists of other normal colours.
Right The Black Short-hair has always been the object of superstition, lucky for some, ill-omened for others.

Above left All cats, even as kittens, are expert climbers, the Short-haired breeds being the more acrobatic.
Left Legend has it that the 'M' mark on the Tabby's forehead was made by the Prophet Mahomet as he stroked the cat.
Above right A Blue-Cream Short-hair grooming her kitten.
Right The established household pet makes the acquaintance of a newcomer.

fact is, however, that if a White cat is born with a few black hairs in its coat breeders regard this as a promising sign, for these hairs will disappear later and, for some inexplicable reason, the cat may not be deaf. White cats with orange or green eyes are likely to have normal hearing and make good pets, even though the latter cannot be entered for shows. Whatever their eye colour, they tend to have exceptionally clean habits and evidently appreciate the patient grooming that is necessary for keeping the coat spotless.

The Short-haired Cream is unfortunately a rare breed, since its coat is expected to be a rich cream, level in

Left A Short-haired Silver Tabby kitten. The ground colour of this breed should be pure silver with distinctive black bands and rings.
Below Bicoloured cat in pensive mood.
Right The head of a British Short-haired cat (of which group the Tabby is typical) is broad, the ears slightly curved and the eyes round and wide open.

colour, free from bars and devoid of white hairs. A discouraging feature from the breeder's point of view is that although kittens frequently fulfil these requirements, faulty bars on the legs and rings on the tail are liable to develop later. The eyes must be copper or hazel.

Probably the most popular of all British Short-haired breeds is the British Blue. This aristocratic-looking cat has a lovely lavender-blue coat which contrasts strikingly with its copper or amber eyes. The colour has been much improved from the earlier dark slate or plum-blue. It is important for show purposes that the coat be really short and soft, not harsh to the touch, and the colour must be perfectly even, without any shading or patches of white. Although the breed is extremely popular in Britain, with a heavy demand for kittens, the British Blue is seldom seen in the United States.

In a very similar breed from France, the Chartreux, the head is not quite so rounded and the standard calls for a coat of any shade of grey or greyish-blue.

Another striking self-coloured Short-haired cat is the Russian Blue. This is one of the Foreign breeds, with a slender, finely-boned body, a flat, narrow skull, a typically wedge-shaped nose and large, pointed ears. The hind legs are longer than those of British Short-haired breeds and the feet are small and oval. Whether it actually originated in Russia is disputed, but some claim that it was once the pet of the Tsars. A previous name for the breed, the Archangel cat, suggests that it may first have been brought into Britain by Russian merchant seamen. To complicate the issue further, in the United States the cat is known as the Maltese.

The special feature of the Russian Blue is its thick coat, as soft and lustrous as sealskin, in a beautiful shade of silver-blue which, for show purposes, must be even all over and quite unmarked. The texture of the coat is quite unlike that of any other cat. The eyes, which are set fairly

This Russian Blue kitten is officially classified as a Foreign Short-haired breed, said to have once been a favourite of the Tsars. The silver-blue coat is thick, soft and lustrous.

wide apart, are almond-shaped and vivid green.

The Russian Blue is intelligent and companionable, with a markedly quieter temperament than other Foreign Short-haired breeds.

Mixing the colours

Bicoloured cats are not very popular at shows, although they are again recognized in Britain as a breed and not just as 'Any other variety'. The second colour, combined with white, may be black, cream, orange or blue.

The Short-haired Blue-Cream is also acceptable as a separate breed. Because such cats are invariably females, careful cross-breeding is necessary between Blues and Creams to produce show specimens. The shape of the body conforms to the standards for the British Blue and the coat colours have to be softly blended, not patched. The eyes must be copper, orange or yellow.

The Short-haired Tortoiseshell is a beautiful cat with a coat containing three colours — black, dark red and cream. This is an extremely difficult cat to breed because the patches on the coat should ideally be clearly defined and unblurred as well as evenly distributed over the whole body, including face, ears, legs, feet and tail. A red blaze is desirable on the face and there must be no hint of white anywhere. The problems of breeding are greatly complicated by the fact that, as with the Long-haired Tortoiseshell, males are sterile, so that a female must be mated with a self-coloured male in one of the acceptable coat colours; and even then the outcome cannot be predicted with any certainty.

Similar difficulties are encountered when trying to breed the Short-haired Tortoiseshell and White or, as it is called in the United States, the Calico cat. Males are extremely rare and the genetic pattern quite unpredictable. In a litter it is unlikely that more than one kitten will possess the same markings as its mother. For exhibition purposes black, dark red, cream and white should be present in clear, brilliant, evenly distributed patches, a patch of white on the back and face being desirable, although the area of white should not be predominant. Eyes must be orange, copper or hazel.

Healthy Exercise

A growing cat needs some form of daily exercise. Not every pet, however, is fortunate enough to live in the country where it can roam through farmyard, field and orchard, free to roll in the grass, climb trees, scale walls and wander about at will, unthreatened by traffic. The town cat is necessarily more restricted but if a garden is available the problem of exercise is automatically solved. All it requires is easy access at all times. If, in the interests of security, you are unable to leave a door or window open you can have a cat door inexpensively fitted to one of the outside doors of the house — a simple swinging flap through which the cat can slip in and out whenever it wishes.

Despite its roving inclinations, however, a cat does not demand as much exercise as a dog. For this reason (and because it is easily housetrained) it is a suitable and popular pet for the flat-dweller, especially for an elderly person. If the flat has a balcony care must be taken to have it safely enclosed. Contrary to what most people believe, the cat does not invariably land on its feet; and despite its quick reactions and flexible limbs it may suffer broken bones or internal injuries if it falls accidentally from a height.

Climbing is the cat's special delight. Even a kitten relishes the challenge of clambering up to a high vantage point and finding its way down again, preferring to walk over chairs, sofas and tables rather than stick to the level floor. Out of doors, where climbing opportunities are many and varied, a cat will always look and think before it leaps, carefully gauging distance or height.

A Tabby surveys his territory from a high vantage point.

Claws may flail as it scrambles up into a tree or onto a fence but once aloft it moves with complete assurance. No tight-wire walker can match the balancing skill of the cat as it delicately treads its way along a swaying branch or a narrow ledge. Even more astonishing is its apparent ability to climb straight up and down. Sometimes it makes a double leap to get up a wall and when descending from a tree often seems to be running right down the vertical trunk. But now and then even a cat miscalculates. Having got up it finds itself stuck. Trapped on a high branch or roof top, it has to be rescued by the fire brigade.

A town cat must be allowed out, whether into the yard or the street, but should be encouraged to stay in at night and, of course, in bad weather. An adult cat may stray some distance and still be experienced enough to find its way home; but a new kitten needs more careful supervision. It is not a bad idea to provide it with a collar and identity disc. Get it accustomed to the strange object by putting it on for a longer period each day; and make sure it has an elastic section so that if it catches on a branch or fence the kitten can easily free itself.

Some owners get their pets used to venturing outdoors by taking them for walks on a lead, attached to a collar or body harness. Certain breeds, such as Siamese, will readily accept the lead if introduced to the concept sufficiently early in life. In the normal course of events a lead is unnecessary; but if you are' in the habit of taking your pet travelling, especially in a car, some form of safe attachment is advisable.

Although some cats welcome a periodic change of surroundings and will let themselves be transported all over the place in a comfortable box or basket, others find travelling an unsettling experience. As a rule it is neither desirable nor practical to take a cat on holiday (going abroad with it is out of the question because of quarantine regulations), so you must make suitable arrangements while you are away. If a friend or neighbour is available to feed and perhaps accommodate it, well and good; but an even better solution is a reputable boarding cattery. The

names of such establishments can be obtained from your vet, from a cat club or from an animal society; and as is the case with good hotels, advance booking is essential. Have a look at the place first. If accommodation is airy and spacious, if the cats already there appear healthy and contented, and if owners and staff take a genuine interest in the dietary needs and special fads and fancies of your pet, you can go away with a clear conscience, knowing that it will be properly looked after.

Cats are by nature inquisitive and adventurous. Although they are remarkably agile they are not invariably accident-proof. But they have a habit of turning up in the most unlikely places.
Left *Cautious descent down a slippery greenhouse roof.*
Above right *View from the top ...*
Below right *... and the bottom.*

Above far left A kitten finds sanctuary among the branches.
Above left Foreign White kitten on the journey up.
Left Burmese kitten almost there.
Right Young Siamese on way down.
Following pages above left Even for a Siamese kitten a wall is no deterrent.
Below left Siamese generally take quite happily to collar and lead.
Right The Chestnut-Brown Foreign or Havana cat, like all Short-haired breeds, needs plenty of exercise.

Long-haired Breeds

The many beautiful Long-haired cats which are so popular on show benches are often referred to as Persians and were at one time known as Angoras. Both names hint at their eastern origins although they do not settle the vexed problem of immediate ancestry. Certainly some of the earliest specimens of long-coated cats to appear in Europe, towards the end of the sixteenth century, were brought in from the Near East and

Below A beautiful pedigree Long-haired Tabby kitten. Colour and pattern are as for Short-haired Tabbies.
Right A seldom seen breed is the Red Self Long-hair. Few females are available and it rarely appears in shows.

the first to be imported into France is said to have come from Angora (Ankara). In Turkey today there is still a blue-eyed cat with long, silky hair which is called the Angora or Ankara cat. It is exhibited from time to time in the United States although no longer seen in Britain.

'Persian' covers a somewhat wider area, but although early breeders definitely imported Long-haired cats from that country there is no reason to think that such animals were restricted to that part of the world. It is generally assumed that these domestic breeds were of central Asiatic origin; but in attempting to trace a common ancestor experts have relied — as in the case of Short-haired cats — on supposition rather than fact. At one time they favoured a small wild cat known, after the man who discovered it, as Pallas's cat, or the manul. This now-rare inhabitant of the plains and deserts of Asia has a broad, flattened head with forward-looking eyes and small ears that are set almost on the same level. The long, soft coat of the manul is silver-grey or buff-yellow with irregular black markings, darker above than below. There are transverse dark streaks on the face and the thick, bushy tail is ringed. Modern authorities see only a superficial resemblance between this fierce little animal and today's domestic Long-haired cat; and indeed recent biological research into the phenomenon of heredity has tended to discredit the theory.

Geography, in fact, no longer has much relevance in this context. The many modern pedigree breeds of Long-hairs, with coat colours in a variety of delicate and subtle shades ranging between the extremes of pure white and jet black, are the products of accidental mating or selective cross-breeding. As with the Short-hairs, new breeds have appeared as a consequence of genetic mutation — unexpected changes in the structure of the sex cells — and it is by a combination of knowledge, experience and, in some situations, trial and error, that a prize-winning pedigree Persian comes to be bred.

The 'cat of contrasts' — a pedigree male Long-haired Smoke.

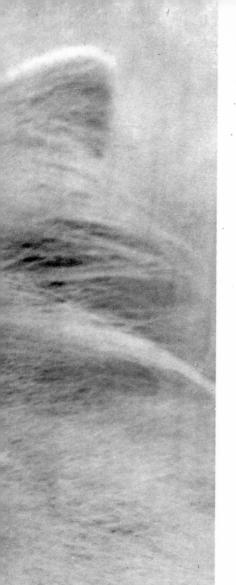

Beauty treatment

The principal distinctive feature of any Persian cat, pedigree or non-pedigree, is its long, flowing, silky coat. This long hair, when brushed back from the neck, forms a handsome frill or ruff which provides an elegant frame for the face and the glittering eyes. Show standards for a Long-haired cat stipulate that the body should be low and stocky, the legs short and thick, the tail short and full. The head is broad and rounded with small, neat ears that should ideally be set rather wide apart. The eyes must be large, round and with a wide-awake look, the nose small and flattened, the cheeks full and the muzzle broad.

Long-haired cats are sometimes accused of being spoiled, indolent creatures, but this is not true. They have no need to be pampered for they are by no means frail or delicate, nor do they require extra care in general upbringing. As a rule their disposition is quite gentle and this docile attitude may be partially responsible for the misconceived belief that they are lazy. The truth is that a Persian spends a greater proportion of its time lying around simply because it is less adventurous and agile than a Short-haired cat, the length of its hair being something of a barrier to rapid movement; but it is every bit as alert, affectionate and intelligent.

For sheer beauty, of course, the Persians are unrivalled, and their visual appeal stems almost wholly from the spick-and-span quality and condition of their fur. The secret of success at shows is patient, expert grooming; but even an ordinary Persian, kept simply as a household pet, needs that extra amount of daily attention if it is to remain clean and healthy. A Long-haired cat with tangled, dirty fur is a sorry sight and there is no excuse for allowing it to get into such a state.

The general procedure for grooming a Long-haired cat is roughly the same as for Short-haired breeds. Daily grooming should ensure that bad matting does not occur; for if the hair is neglected, causing mats and tangles to form, these have to be cut away with round-ended scissors. Removal of these lumps of fur will leave a ragged, untidy effect for a while but the hair soon grows once more. Such a drastic remedy is, however, unnecessary if the cat is combed and brushed thoroughly all over, with particular attention being paid to the back legs and tail — those areas where knots may most easily accumulate. One essential difference in grooming Persians is that brushing or hand-stroking the fur should be carried out in the opposite direction to that adopted for Short-haired cats — upward towards the head — so that the frill stands erect and is not flattened down.

Another important reason why Long-haired cats require more thorough grooming is that they are more likely to swallow fur balls, especially when they are moulting. A cat that grooms itself in the normal way is liable to swallow a little hair but this is usually eliminated in the normal course of nature. Sometimes, however, the stomach becomes distended as a result of too much fur accumulating and medical or surgical treatment may be necessary. Frequent grooming to remove all loose hair will reduce the chance of this happening.

Black, white and silver

The principal breeds of Long-haired cats recognized in Britain for show purposes are: Black, Blue-eyed White, Orange-eyed White, Odd-eyed White, Chinchilla, Blue, Red Self, Cream, Blue-Cream, Smoke, Silver Tabby, Brown Tabby, Red Tabby, Tortoiseshell, Tortoiseshell and White, Colourpoint and Bicoloured. The American Cat Fancy, however, recognizes a number of other breeds, including the Shaded Silver and variously coloured Cameos.

The Long-haired Black cat, still carrying superstitious overtones, is one of the oldest pedigree breeds but is not nowadays seen so frequently in shows. One reason may be that the kittens are less attractive than those of other self-coloured breeds. In the

Left Face of a Champion — Archsue Barwell Clary, Cream Long-hair.
Following pages above left A family of Colourpoints.
Below left A well groomed Orange-eyed Persian.
Right The Long-haired Black cat is one of the oldest pedigree breeds.

Left The delicate colour effect of this Long-haired Smoke kitten is achieved by the contrasting white undercoat and black topcoat shading to silver.
Below left The Chinchilla, with its pure white undercoat and black-tipped white topcoat, is one of the loveliest of cats.
Right A non-pedigree ginger Persian with outsize whiskers.
Far right Geneticists have now evolved a formula for breeding pedigree Long-haired Blue-Creams.
Below right An appealing trio of Persian cats — Chinchilla, Black and Smoke.

first few months of life they are likely to be brownish-grey rather than black and only in adult life will their true beauty become evident. The colour may, in fact, remain rusty up to the age of five or six months; yet such kittens may eventually develop the densest black colour and thus be ideal for showing. At birth the undercoat may be whitish but this too will later disappear.

Standards for this breed call for a lustrous, raven-black coat, free from rustiness, shading, marking or flecks of white; and the eyes must be copper or deep orange with no trace of green around the rim. As with the Short-haired Black, this coat colour is very easily spoiled so that it must not be allowed to get wet or be exposed to very strong sunlight. Some people

Left The Blue-Cream Persian goes by the alternative name of Blue Tortoiseshell.
Below left This mother and her kitten are Red Self Long-hairs, known in the United States either as Solid Reds or as Red Persians.
Right Grooming session for a White Persian.
Below right Long-haired Red Tabby.

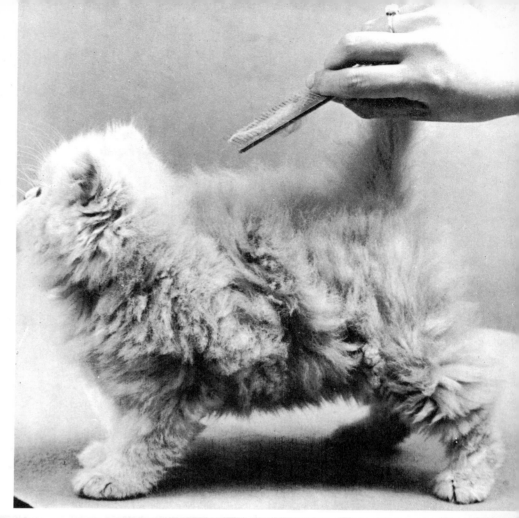

still regard this breed as the most handsome of all, and there is no denying the lovely contrasting effect of the round, orange eyes against the jet black face and frill.

Long-haired Blue-eyed Whites were probably first introduced from Asia into France and from there to many parts of Europe and overseas. Nowadays they are comparatively rare. Their major disadvantage is that, as is the case with their Short-haired cousins, a great many of them grow up to be incurably deaf. Few of them have perfect hearing. It is possible that this defect is due to partial albinism, for although true albinos are rare in the cat world, deafness is a feature of this condition. Moreover, the fact that the blue eyes sometimes give out a reddish glint when seen in certain lights provides some support for the theory.

It was in their attempts to eliminate this defect and improve coat colour that breeders introduced other cats into their mating pattern, including Blacks, Blues and Creams, all with orange eyes. The result, in many cases, was a white cat with orange eyes; and in 1960 the Orange-eyed White was registered in Britain by the Governing Council of the Cat Fancy as an independent breed. Since then Orange-eyed Whites have been more common than Blue-eyed Whites and because they are not prone to deafness have often been used as mates for Blue-eyed White females. Sometimes the result has been a kitten with one blue eye and one orange eye — the so-called Odd-eyed White. Although long recognized in America as a separate breed, it has only recently been registered in Britain. To complicate matters still further for the breeder, all white kittens at birth have blue eyes and only at about eight weeks does the permanent adult eye colour become evident.

Long-haired Whites require the most thorough grooming, twice a day if necessary, in order to attain the immaculate coat colour demanded for showing. As if aware of their beauty, they spend a good deal of time washing and cleaning themselves. Show standards require

dignified non-pedigree Tabby and White kitten.

the coat to be pure white, without marking or shading of any kind, and the major risk is that yellow tints may develop, especially around the tail, as a result of mud or grease. Males seem to be more prone to this soiling than females. Dirt and grease can be removed from the coat with powder and careful brushing, but since flecks of powder may be grounds for disqualification at a show, this must always be done several days in advance. The hair, as with all Long-haired breeds, must be soft and silky, not woolly in texture, and the brush full.

Many of the Orange-eyed Whites fall short of perfection in respect of eye colour, for a really vivid orange is not easy to obtain; but many excellent show specimens are nowadays being bred, notably in France and Britain.

An even more beautiful breed of Long-haired cat is the Chinchilla. Authors describing this cat seldom seem to be able to avoid epithets such as 'ethereal' and 'fairy-like'; and its principal attraction is its purity of colouring. As a kitten the Chinchilla (which, incidentally, has no connection with the Andean rodent of the same name) has faint tabby markings on legs and tail, but these gradually disappear as it grows and eventually the beautiful, pure white undercoat emerges.

Each white hair of the topcoat is tipped with black and this gives the breed its distinctive sparkling silver appearance. This tipping or ticking must be clear and even over the shoulders, back, head, flanks and tail and can only be seen to best advantage as a result of attentive grooming, when the undercoat shows through. Otherwise the hairs of the topcoat are inclined to lie too flat and the ticking will give a darker overall effect than is ideally required for exhibition purposes.

The tabby markings visible in the Chinchilla kitten arise from the fact that the breed is thought to have originated from a crossing of the Long-haired Silver Tabby and the Tortoiseshell and White. Chinchillas are not very prolific nor are good show specimens easy to breed. This is hardly surprising when one considers the very rigid standards required — pure white undercoat and absolutely

even ticking to provide the beautiful silvery sheen. The ticking may extend, though to a lesser degree, to the legs; but the chin, ear tufts, stomach and chest have to be pure white. No tabby markings or brown or cream tinges are permissible. The tip of the nose has to be brick-red and the visible skin on eyelids and pads black or dark brown. The coat, of course, must be fine and silky in texture and extra long on the frill. The eyes should be emerald or blue-green. Although at one time any eye colour, including brown, was permitted, this is no longer the case.

Breeders have recently produced interesting and beautiful variations of the standard Chinchilla, such as the Shaded Silver, the Masked Silver and the Cameos, none of which are thus far recognized in Britain. Some breeders have also tried crossing the Chinchilla with a Blue Persian in order to produce the Blue Chinchilla, with a coat that is ticked with blue instead of black.

Prides of the show

Regarded by many cat-lovers as the king of the show is the Blue Persian, which has been bred in Britain for some eighty-five years and is in great demand among overseas buyers. The silky quality of its coat is such that it is often used for improving the standard of other Long-haired breeds. This cat is somewhat larger than the Long-haired Whites and this alone tends to give it an authoritarian appearance.

The body of the Blue Persian should be cobby, not too long, with short, thick legs; the head broad with a good space between the tiny, well tufted ears which are set well down on either side; the nose short and broad; and the eyes large, wide open and coloured copper or orange, with no trace of green. The coat has to be long, thick and soft, with a full frill around the head. The standard allows the coat to be any shade of blue, and this may range from palest lavender to deepest sapphire. The paler shades have the disadvantage, however, of being subject to damage under strong sunlight. The blue, whether light, medium or dark, must be sound and even, free from markings, shading or white hairs; and the frill must be exactly the same colour as the fur on the

Left Despite its charm, this kitten does not qualify as a registered breed.
Below left The Colourpoint, basically the same breed as the Himalayan cat of the United States, is a Persian with Siamese colouring.
Right The Long-haired Smoke is unfortunately a vanishing breed.
Below right The flowing coat of the Cream Long-hair is delicate ivory in colour. If the fur is red-tinged the colour is described as 'hot', this being undesirable by show standards.

Above Who said Persians were lazy? This Red kitten can climb with the best.
Left In the Blue-Cream Long-hair coat colours are softly intermingled.
Above right The pale colour of the Cream Long-hair is obtained by mating Creams with Blues.
Right Study in extremes — a Long-haired White and a Long-haired Black kitten. The blue eyes of the latter show that it is still very young. All kittens are born with blue eyes.
Following pages left Long-haired cats enjoy playing in the grass but that extra bit of care is needed to keep the fur as clean as this.
Above right Close-up of a prize-winning Blue Persian.
Below right The Long-haired Blue-eyed White cat is frequently handicapped by imperfect hearing.

rest of the body. Another definite fault is a kink in the tail, which should be short and very full.

A Blue Persian kitten may display tabby markings when born but, as with most other self-coloured breeds, these disappear in later life.

A very much rarer breed, seldom seen in shows anywhere, is the Long-haired Red Self, known in the United States as the Red Persian or the Solid Red. The deep, rich red colour required is infrequently attained, for the tabby markings seen in the kittens do not always vanish and even when the body is clear there may be faulty streaks on the head. An additional problem in breeding the Red Self is that few females are available.

Much commoner, and very popular, is the Cream, its deep copper eyes shining like tiny jewels against the ivory colour of the long, flowing fur. The coat should ideally be pure and sound throughout, free of markings, and each hair unshaded from root to tip. The colour should be a cool cream rather than too red, when it is described as 'hot'. This deeper shade, regarded as a fault, tends to coarsen the hair which should, of course, be dense and silky. The breed was apparently produced by mating Blue males with Red females, but in order to prevent the 'hot' colour appearing, breeders now try to retain the paler colour by mating Creams with Blues.

Formula for breeding

The Long-haired Blue-Cream is becoming increasingly popular and represents a real challenge to breeders. It is a cross between Blue and Cream Long-hairs, and geneticists have worked out a formula so that the coloration of the offspring can be predicted. This colour inheritance is one of the rare examples of so-called sex linkage in animals. When a Cream male is mated to a Blue female the resulting male kittens will be Blue, the females Blue-Cream. A Blue male crossed with a Cream female will similarly produce Blue-Cream female kittens

This charming Long-haired White kitten may grow up to become a Champion, but constant care will be required to prevent any part of the pure white fur turning a yellowish colour.

but Cream males. A Blue-Cream female mated to a Blue male could have Blue or Cream males and Blue or Blue-Cream females; but if the father is Cream the colour pattern will be partially reversed, with Blue or Cream males and Cream or Blue-Cream females. It will be noted that in such litters there will seldom be any Blue-Cream males; if they do survive they are invariably sterile and thus of no value for breeding.

Another difficulty in breeding Blue-Creams is that the colours, at any rate in Britain and the Continent, should be softly intermingled to give the hazy appearance of shot silk. In the United States, however, the blues and creams may appear in solid patches, explaining why the breed is known in that country as the Blue Tortoiseshell. The two colours should be pale pastel, without any hint of red. The eyes should be deep copper or orange. Blue-Cream kittens are enchanting, with a keen sense of fun; and even if small colour patches on legs, face or head spoil the show chances of an otherwise perfect cat, this breed makes a placid and charming household companion.

Tabbies and Tortoiseshells

Show cats are subject to the whims of fashion and the Long-haired Smoke is a breed whose popularity is on the wane. Recognized in two colours, Black and Blue, it is referred to as a 'cat of contrasts', the delicate effect being created by the pure white undercoat and the black (or blue) topcoat, shading to silver on the sides. Eyes should be orange or copper; mask and feet must be black, frill and ear tufts silver. The pale undercoat is clearly visible as the cat moves. Show specimens require the most careful grooming if the coat is not to become shabby. Kittens of this hardy breed are born black and the lighter undercoat is only seen after several weeks.

The Long-haired Tabbies are seen (though infrequently) in the same three colours as the Short-haired varieties — Silver, Brown and Red. The Long-haired Silver Tabby is extremely elegant but unfortunately very rare. The ground colour should ideally be pale silver (not brindled or grey), with dense and distinct black markings, exactly as for striped and blotched Short-haired Tabbies. The

true tabby markings should be very plainly seen and not run into one another, as is frequently the case. Because the long, flowing coat tends to obscure the pattern, the fur is usually kept very smooth, being brushed in both directions, from shoulder to tail and from shoulder to head.

A good Long-haired Brown Tabby is also difficult to breed, mainly because the show standards require the coat to be rich tawny sable with dense black markings conforming to a definite pattern. This includes the distinctive butterfly markings on the shoulders, regular striping on the legs and the tail, delicate pencilling on the face and two or three swirls on the cheeks.

The Long-haired Red Tabby is equally a challenge to breeders with its deep, rich red ground colour and bold, clear tabby markings. One fault which is especially hard to eradicate is a white tip to the tail.

The two related breeds, Long-haired Tortoiseshell and Long-haired Tortoiseshell and White (or Calico) are comparatively rare for the same reasons as apply to the similarly coloured Short-haired breeds. In the first place it is hard to obtain the correct, distinct and evenly distributed colour patching (black, red and cream in the former instance, with the addition of white in the latter breed); secondly, males of these two breeds are notoriously rare, the tortoiseshell colouring being transferred to female kittens only. When males do appear they are invariably sterile.

In Britain the basic colours of the Tortoiseshell and White have to be distinctly patched and interspersed with white. The American Cat Fanciers' Association stipulates that one side of the face should be black, the other red or cream. The white areas are expected to be limited only to certain areas of the body, so that the Calico cat has the appearance of having been dipped in a can of white paint.

Best of both worlds

One of the Long-haired breeds which has received official recognition only quite recently is the Colourpoint. This is a perfect example of selective breeding — a cat with the unique markings of a Siamese (a Foreign

Short-hair) and the fur and body shape of a typical Persian.

For some years prior to the Second World War breeders in several countries carried out experiments with various Siamese and Persian cats in endeavours to produce a genuine Long-haired Siamese. Up to a point they were successful, for although the offspring of such matings failed to show the typical Siamese markings they carried the gene for the Siamese coat pattern and this would often appear when the kittens grew and were mated with one another. The trouble was, however, that these cats with their slender, streamlined bodies looked awkward and unattractive with Persian-type long hair.

Experiments continued in Britain after the war, the aim being to transfer the delicate Siamese colouring, yet at the same time to eliminate the familiar Siamese body shape. By crossing selected Long-haired Siamese with the finest available Persians, kittens were in due course produced with precisely the qualities desired — Siamese colouring and Persian fur and body type.

Show standards require the Colourpoint to be cobby, low on the legs, with a broad, round head, widely placed, small, tufted ears, a short nose and well developed cheeks. The eyes must be bright and deep blue. The tail should be short and full, without a kink. The fur must be long, thick and soft, the frill full. Four Siamese colourings are acceptable — Seal Point, Lilac Point, Blue Point or Chocolate Point, with the appropriate Siamese body colour — cream, glacial white, ivory or magnolia respectively. Points must be solid in colour and matched by body shading, if any should occur.

Not all the difficulties have been solved. Many Colourpoints have pale blue eyes rather than the lovely sapphire-blue eyes of the Siamese; and the eyes are often not large or round enough to conform to the Persian standard. The perfect specimen, however, is a cat of spectacular beauty.

Another reason for its popularity is that, although of Siamese stock, the Colourpoint has not inherited the rather noisy, demanding attitude of its ancestors and shows no signs of being highly strung. It is hardy, gentle

and affectionate, and does not object to being picked up and handled. As with all Long-haired cats, the fur must be carefully and thoroughly groomed for it to appear to the best advantage.

In the United States the Himalayan cat is virtually the same as the British Colourpoint, but whereas only four of the Siamese colourings are recognized in Britain the American Cat Fancy classifies two more — Red Point and Frost Point.

Return to favour
In early shows cats with two distinct coat colours were not uncommon, but later they lost their popularity and were dropped from the list of registered breeds. Now they are once more recognized in combinations of black and white (familiarly called Magpies), blue and white, red and white, and cream and white. Standards for colour are identical to those applying to their Short-haired counterparts and the pattern demanded by show judges is exacting. The two colours must appear in equal amounts, evenly broken on body and face, and with no tabby markings on the self-coloured portions. Shoulders, neck, forelegs, feet, chin and lips should ideally be white; and there should be a white blaze up the face and over the top of the head. Thus although the mask is self-coloured, the white blaze divides the face exactly in half. Other self-coloured parts are the ears, the hind legs (but not the feet) and the tail. It is obvious that breeding a cat with such precise colour definitions is far from simple.

Above right Long-haired Red Tabby.
Right Long-haired Silver Tabby.

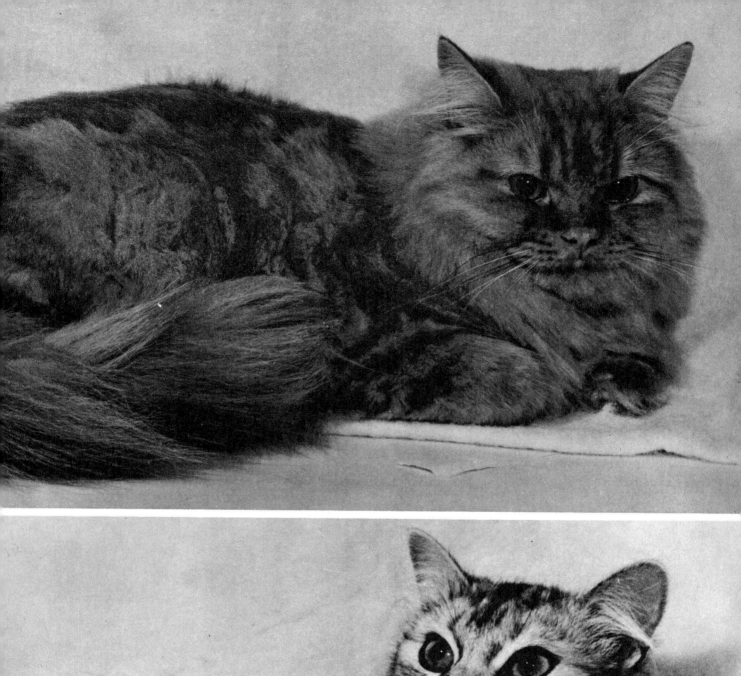

Playtime

The instinct to play is deeply rooted in all baby animals. It is delightfully evident from the moment the kitten begins to totter around, exploring its surroundings and suddenly discovering the presence of other creatures of the same size and shape that appear to be similarly disposed. In fact a kitten will put so much determination and concentrated energy into every minute of its waking hours that it will very quickly tire. Almost without warning it will nod off. A little later and just as suddenly, it will wake up, have a good stretch and be off on its antics again.

A kitten is capable of amusing itself with the simplest kind of playthings — bits of string, pieces of paper, scraps of felt, reels of cotton, spools of wool, pingpong balls, catnip mice and the like. You may be tempted to provide your pet with more expensive, elaborate toys but, as happens with children, these are quite likely to be left untouched. Do not, in any event, give a kitten any toy made of rubber or plastic nor, of course, anything with dangerously sharp points or edges.

Objects that can change shape and which are made of materials into which it can sink its claws are particularly appreciated. A small stuffed toy may divert a kitten for hours, and it is most entertaining to watch it as it tosses its imaginary enemy in the air or tramples it, growling, underfoot. Sometimes it will perform the most graceful ballet movements, leaping high through space, as it plays. Obviously it appreciates an audience and

Above *You may wonder why I stand before you today …*
Right *Straight left to the jaw.*
Far right *Enough to make you cross-eyed.*

Left A compact ball of string ...
Right ... is more·fun when unravelled.
Below Friendly rough-and-tumble.

Left *A simple toy is best.*
Right *Tabby tangle.*
Below *Should I kick it?*

will indulge in ever more complex and skilful dance movements if it is conscious that you are watching. It is quite astonishing, too, to see to what imaginative use a kitten can put a simple cardboard box or a paper (but on no account a plastic) bag.

As a newcomer to the household a kitten will expect you to provide the security and loving comfort it originally received from its mother. Allowing it to lie peacefully in your lap and caressing it gently by stroking its head with your finger will help to reassure it and make it feel wanted. Do not attempt to hold it against its will. Play with it when it seems so in-clined but let it sleep as soon as it shows signs of tiring.

Small children in the house have to be taught to treat a kitten gently and not expect it to join in all their forms of rough and tumble, for its limbs are extremely fragile. It will probably be quite happy following a piece of string trailed across the floor or trying to trap a ball. Best of all is to allow it to devise its own games, preferably with another kitten as playmate.

As it grows older and more experienced the cat may well tire of these simple games, but it will never completely lose its sense of fun. Now, however, its greatest pleasure may come from activities seemingly un-connected with play as we under-stand it. Stalking birds in the garden may be one such source of enjoy-ment and although you may dis-approve you cannot do anything to stop it.

It is a delusion to think that because a cat happens to follow a par-ticular instruction it is going to obey you on every occasion and in every situation. The only reason it falls in with your wishes is that it suits its purpose to do so. Do not expect a cat to show off for your entertainment. It is quite against its nature to per-

form tricks and it would be foolish on your part to encourage it to act uncharacteristically. Many a cat will, of course, pick up what appear to be clever knacks such as opening doors and pressing bells, but such actions bring about tangible results, namely to get in and out.

The refusal of a cat to perform tricks, like dogs and other animals that are paraded in circuses, has nothing to do with lack of intelligence. Indeed one could argue that in declining to cooperate it is showing uncommon sense. Its very indifference is the despair of those who would test animal intelligence by subjecting them to tests involving mazes, colour cards and selected stimulants. In the sense of using its brains to bring about a desired objective — surely a more valid criterion than getting it to stand on its head or balance a ball on its nose — the cat is undoubtedly an intelligent animal.

Below left This cat evidently aspires to be a ballet dancer.
Right Order of the boot.
Below Wrestling match for a pair of Abyssinians.

Favourites from the East

Legends would have us believe that the enormously popular Siamese cat was at one time worshipped in Buddhist temples and that the breed was treasured in the royal palace at Bangkok. According to the latter story, the cats acted as the repositories for the souls of departed kings, being buried with them in their tombs. When the cat escaped through a small hole left in the roof it was assumed that the soul's transference had taken place and the animal was henceforth honoured as if royal blood ran in its own veins.

Without doubt there is a regal air to the Siamese cat which suggests there could be some truth in these stories, and although neither really stands up to close examination, especially the former, no harm is done by giving them credibility. There is reason to believe that the cats were highly valued (and, presumably, very expensive) in Siam as pets before making their appearance in the West and that they were kept by royalty, with harsh punishments exacted for stealing them.

During the late nineteenth century the King of Siam, Rama V, seems to have been sufficiently concerned about the future of the breed to permit only a few trusted foreigners to take the cats, particularly males, out of his country. But the fact that the cats which later became generally known as Siamese were actually exported from that country does not mean that Thailand, as it is now called, was the only land of origin. It is interesting to note, for example, that the Thais sometimes refer to this breed as the 'Chinese' cat, which

Below A Lilac Point Siamese queen. This is one of the newer colour types, known in the United States as the Frost Point.
Right Grace and agility are hallmarks of the Siamese cat.

leaves room for speculation.

Nevertheless it was the King of Siam who, in 1884, made his first official gift of a pair of Siamese cats to Mr Owen Gould, then British Consul-General in Bangkok. Mr Gould apparently handed over these cats to his sister, Mrs Veley, a breeder who exhibited them at the Crystal Palace Show the following year and subsequently, in 1901, became a founder member in Britain of the Siamese Cat Club. Accounts do not agree as to whether she actually bred from this first pair or from later arrivals, but enough Siamese cats were brought into the country during the next decade or so for the breed to become firmly established; and in 1892 a standard of points for Siamese cats was published in *Our Cats*.

There are conflicting claims as to who was the first owner of a Siamese cat in North America. The earliest imported specimens arrived in 1895 and the breed was being regularly exhibited and winning prizes in the first decade of the present century. The Siamese Cat Club of America was founded in 1909.

It has been reported that Siamese cats were being smuggled aboard ships from the Far East some time before 1884 and there are written descriptions and drawings to suggest that the breed was already familiar in Europe in the first half of the nineteenth century. The cats may even have been on display at the first Crystal Palace Show of 1871. The likelihood is that Siamese reached foreign ports as ordinary ships' cats, arousing polite interest by reason of their unusual shape and colouring but not being taken up seriously by breeders until they began to be legally imported from the Orient during the 1880s.

The distant descendants of these early Siamese, most of which, incidentally, were Seal Pointed, are now distributed all over the world, and selective breeding has produced a number of beautiful new colour types.

The Siamese cat is a deservedly popular pet. Although inclined to be noisy and demanding at times, it is intelligent, playful, affectionate and, needless to add, very handsome.

The cat that is different

The principal reason for the immense popularity enjoyed by the Siamese cat, apart from its singular beauty and elegance, is that it also possesses a highly individual character. It really is a cat with a difference. Many people who tend to object to cats on the grounds that they are inclined to be aloof and unfriendly quickly warm to the Siamese because it measures up to their expectation of what a real pet should be — affectionate and loyal. Not that the Siamese would consider it a compliment to be compared with a dog. Indeed it differs from a dog in one important respect — it is not slavishly obedient. Even a Siamese kitten makes it understood from the start that it possesses a will of iron.

In assessing the very special character of the Siamese cat it would be foolish to overlook its faults. Not even the most obsessive owner would claim it is perfect in every respect. It is undeniably noisy, inclined to be nervous and highly strung, and occasionally very destructive. Unforgiving critics accuse it, too, of being greedy, self-centred, jealous and much more besides. But the countless owners who have long since succumbed to the singular charms of the Siamese are not unduly troubled by such condemnations. In their eyes any such minor faults are far outweighed by the attractions of the breed — humour, playfulness, intelligence, expressiveness, courage, fidelity, companionship and deep affection. Own a Siamese and you can give allegiance to no other breed.

A Siamese kitten will have no qualms about making its feelings and needs known as soon as it is old enough to stand up, start showing normal curiosity and take interest in its surroundings. It may immediately announce its individuality by refusing to eat the foods recommended in the manuals for other cats. The unacceptable items of the diet may include raw meat or, more commonly, milk. In both kittens and cats milk may cause diarrhoea and should on no account be forced. The kitten may go further and embark on a total hunger strike but this must be rectified as soon as possible. The secret at this stage is firmness, even if it develops into a battle of wills. The kitten must

be trained during these early weeks to accept a mixed diet, although only patient trial and error will indicate which foods it likes and dislikes. There can be a good deal of flexibility in preparing menus but two basic rules should be observed at all times. Do not over-feed and do not pamper. Once you give in to all its whims you will find yourself landed with an autocrat around the house.

A Siamese cat craves love and attention more than any other breed. Provided the necessary introductions are made sufficiently early in life, it will get on well with other cats and with dogs as well; but more important is the constant need for close human contact. It is not simply the instinctive demand of all cats for food and warmth; it is a positive entreaty to be kept occupied and entertained. Leave a Siamese alone for any length of time and it will quickly become bored, dejected, even ill; and it does not throw off illness lightly. It may announce its displeasure by giving vent to the raucous howling (not unlike that of a yelling child) that is such a distinctive feature of the breed and the cause of its unpopularity in certain circles; and if loneliness is the cause it will get into mischief, deliberately looking for objects to tear up or destroy. One thing is sure. It is not just exercising its vocal cords for nothing. The range of sounds emitted will be subtly varied, not necessarily unpleasing to the ear, and the experienced owner will soon know precisely what all this 'talking' signifies — pain, hunger, plain boredom or sexual interest — and will react accordingly. If it is caused by a physical ailment seek professional advice at once. The Siamese needs immediate expert treatment for it makes a poor invalid; but its recovery will be all the quicker if you remain around to assure it of your love and concern.

Part of a cat's charm is the fact that it is not exactly like any other, either in looks or behaviour. This is even truer of the Siamese which, for all its loyalty and devotion, retains its right to be aloof, solitary and mysterious if so inclined. It commands respect and admiration as well as love; and only somebody who has owned one can fully understand and appreciate its unique qualities.

Left The Red Abyssinian, known in the United States as the Sorrel, has a beautiful copper-red coat.

Right The Burmese cat is more placid than the Siamese but equally lively and intelligent.

Below The Seal Point Siamese was the first type to be imported to Europe from the Far East.

Following pages above left The coat of the Blue Point Siamese is glacial white with slate-blue points.

Below left A Lilac Point mother and kitten. This type of Siamese is a cross between a Blue Point and Chocolate Point.

Right The coat of the Brown Burmese is glossy, close-lying and fine in texture.

Points that count

Siamese cats are classified as a Foreign Short-haired breed and the several recognized varieties differ from one another basically in the colour of their 'points' — the dark markings which are superimposed on the light body colour. These appear on the mask, ears, feet and tail, all in a matching tone. On the face the mask spreads out over the cheeks and up over the forehead to the base of the ears.

Official standards for pedigree Siamese have gradually changed over the years, for the earliest show specimens had a rounded rather than a pointed face as well as a darker coat. Today's standards call for a long, slender body with well-shaped back and haunches, and hind legs that are slightly longer than the forelegs, producing an upward-sloping effect. The feet must be delicate and oval in shape. The head is narrow and wedge-shaped, tapering smoothly in a straight line to the muzzle, with rather large ears set well apart, wide at the base, pointed at the tips, and pricked. There should also be a generous width between the eyes which are brilliant blue and almond-shaped, with no squint. The long slim tail should taper to a point and not be too thick at the root. A slight kink at the extremity of the tail used to be acceptable but is not nowadays liked at shows. There is a charming story about how this kink (a common feature) originated. A Siamese princess once went bathing and hung her rings on her favourite cat's tail, tying a knot at the end to prevent them slipping off. When she untied the knot the slight kink remained.

Male Siamese are fairly heavy cats and are normally somewhat larger than the females, but the overall appearance of the body should be sleek and elegant and not too corpulent. Breeding queens should not be too small since the chances are that such cats will give birth to thin, scrawny kittens which may turn out to be nervy and have little resistance to illness.

In the United States the standards for Siamese are slightly different, favouring a longer, thinner body and even narrower head. Many experts consider the effect unattractive, the risk being that the good, unreceding chin shape may be lost.

Still the most popular Siamese is the original breed — the Seal Pointed Siamese, known more simply as the Seal Point. Standards require the mask, ears, legs, feet and tail to be rich seal-brown, without brindling. As in all colour varieties, the coat must be close-lying, short and fine. The ideal coat colour is cream, shading to pale fawn on the back and to creamy white on the belly and chest. The kittens, like those of other Siamese, are almost white when born and the characteristic points only become visible as the animals grow. The connecting lines between mask and ears may not be apparent until the cat is adult. The eyes must be clear and brilliant blue.

Because all Siamese kittens are born white, identification is sometimes only possible by examining the pads of the feet — dark brown in the Seal Point, grey in the Blue Point, pale brown in the Chocolate Point and pinkish or frosty grey in the Lilac Point.

Brindling in the colour of the points, perhaps as a result of illness or a long spell of hot weather, is regarded as a fault; so too are light paws and chin. Another feature that may spoil the cat's show chances is a dark patch underneath, known as a 'belly spot'.

Although the Blue Pointed Siamese was first bred in Britain in 1894 it was only registered by the Cat Fancy as a separate colour in 1936. The body colour is described as glacial white (with no fawn), shading gradually into blue on the back, which should be of a lighter shade than the slate-blue of the points. The colour of the eyes should be brilliant blue but not quite as deep as that of the Seal Point.

Owners and breeders of Siamese insist that the characters of differently pointed cats vary distinctly and that the Blue Point is much gentler and less aggressive than the Seal Point.

The first Chocolate Point was imported into Britain a few years before the turn of the last century but remained comparatively rare for some time, gaining official recognition in 1951. It is one of the loveliest varieties, with an ivory coat (without shading) and milk-chocolate points (lighter than the Seal Point colour-ing). The eyes are a bright vivid blue. The only permissible shading is in the colour of the points. It is a difficult cat to breed and its temperament too is noticeably quieter than that of the Seal Point.

The Lilac Point, recognized in Britain in 1961 and known in the United States as the Frost Point, is a cross between a Blue Point and a Chocolate Point, sometimes appearing unexpectedly in litters where the parents carry both blue and chocolate factors. Numbers are on the increase since Lilac Points always breed true to colour. The coat is frosty-grey (almost white), the points pale pinkish-mauve and the eyes vivid blue. It too has a soft, gentle nature.

As a result of experimental breeding (mating with British Short-hairs) new colour points have appeared in recent years and have received official recognition. The Red Point, for example, is a very beautiful Siamese, with a gentle, affectionate nature. Its body colour is white, shading on the back to apricot; the points are reddish-gold and the eyes brilliant blue. Signs of its Red Tabby ancestry are sometimes evident in the faint tabby markings on the face and it is not always easy to eliminate the rings on the tail.

The Tabby Pointed Siamese is also an attractive cat which makes no secret of its origin. The first Tabby Points were the result of an accidental mating between a Seal Point female and a Tabby male. Because the gene for tabby is dominant it is

Previous pages above left Three six-month-old Red Point Siamese kittens. Show specimens should have no rings on the tail.
Below left At four days old all that these Chocolate Point Siamese kittens want to do is feed and sleep.
Above right Two Abyssinian kittens go exploring and find a Spaniel.
Below right The tabby markings on these Abyssinian kittens will gradually fade as they grow older.
Opposite above A female Abyssinian scaling a fence. Although the first specimen actually came from Abyssinia, today's cats are the product of selective breeding in the West.
Right The most unusual type of Siamese is the Tortie Point. The tortoiseshell colouring appears on face and paws.

not easy to get rid of tabby markings in many self-coloured breeds, but in this case a deliberate attempt was made to transfer the pattern to the points of a Siamese. The pale beauty of the coat and the pencilled tabby markings of the points create a delightful effect and the kittens are especially enchanting. Standards require the tabby markings on the mask, particularly around the nose, eyes and cheeks, to be clearly defined and the whisker pads to be darkly spotted. Broken stripes can appear on the legs but the backs of the hind legs should be solidly marked (so that the cats seem to be wearing black stockings), as should the ears. The tail is ringed, ending in a solid tip.

The same carefully planned breeding programme applies to the quaintest of all Siamese, the Tortie Point. The body of this breed is cream to fawn, with shading to match the basic tortoiseshell colouring of the points. The ears are a mixture of seal-brown and red, the mask a blend (in equal proportions) of seal-brown and cream, sometimes with a sprinkling of red; the legs and feet should be marbled with red or ivory, or both. In this breed, as in the true Tortoiseshells and Tortoiseshell and Whites, most kittens prove to be females which, mated to males of a basic colour, may produce variously pointed Siamese.

The docile Abyssinian

In 1869 the wife of a British army officer serving in Abyssinia brought to Britain a sleek, short-haired cat which bore a striking resemblance to the cats of ancient Egyptian frescoes and bronzes. This was the first specimen seen in Europe of a breed which, for the sake of convenience rather than accuracy, became known as the Abyssinian. Whether it is a true descendant of the wild caffre cat or in any way related to the domestic cat worshipped in ancient Egypt will probably never be resolved. The fact that there are no cats of this type in Ethiopia today hardly reinforces the theory that the breed originated in that part of the world; and in any event, the modern Abyssinian is en-

Feline strength and grace are epitomized in this Brown Burmese cat, silhouetted here against the sky.

tirely the product of selective breeding in Britain. First exhibited at the Crystal Palace Show of 1883 and not introduced into the United States for another fifty years or so, this charming little cat is now deservedly a popular favourite.

The Abyssinian is classified as a Foreign Short-haired type and although it has the elongated body and slender bones common to such breeds it is distinguished by the highly unusual colour and pattern of its coat. Whereas in the majority of cats intermingled hairs of varied colours appear in the coat, each hair of the Abyssinian's coat is ticked with two or three separate bands of colour. The ground colour is rich russet-brown and the individual bands are dark brown or black. The only exceptions are the hairs of the belly and inside of the forelegs which do not have more than a single band. It is this dark tipping or ticking which gives the coat its special quality; and because the colouring is similar to that of a wild rabbit the Abyssinian is sometimes known as the 'bunny' cat.

The body of the Abyssinian should be fairly long and lithe, but muscular, the head long and pointed, the ears sharp (though not as long as those of the Siamese) and comparatively broad at the base. The eyes are required to be large, bright and expressive, in green, yellow or hazel. The black-tipped tail must be fairly long and tapering but thicker at the root than that of the Siamese. The fur should be fine and close, soft and silky in texture yet springy to the touch.

In the original breed — the Normal Abyssinian — each hair has to be ticked, preferably with two or three

dark brown or black bands, separated by the ground colour of ruddy-brown. The hair of the belly and inside of the forelegs should blend with the main body colour, for preference orange-brown and unmarked. A dark line running up the spine is not considered a fault but any tabby markings and bars on head, legs and tail lose points at shows and may even be grounds for disqualification. Another common fault, difficult to eliminate, is any white marking around the chin and throat. Ideally the chin should be cream. The pads of the feet are black and this colour should extend up the back of the hind legs. extend up the back of the hind

Some of the early breeders of Abyssinians were occasionally worried, and doubtless annoyed, by the fact that in certain litters kittens would appear with the wrong coat colour — too much red to merit the description ruddy-brown. More and more of these abnormal kittens were born until they were eventually recognized as a separate breed. The coat of the Red Abyssinian (known in the United States as the Sorrel) is solid copper-red, with each hair doubly or trebly ticked with contrasting darker (but not black) bands. The hairs of the belly should be deep apricot. Eye colour is the same as for the Normal Abyssinian but the pads of the feet are pink. Tail and ears should be tipped in dark brown.

The Abyssinian is not a prolific breed. A female will have a small litter, normally not exceeding four kittens, most of which will be males. Numbers being relatively few, there are long waiting lists for kittens. The adult Abyssinian is hardy and appreciates plenty of freedom. Active and very playful, it can be trained to the collar and lead and will emulate a dog in bringing back objects tossed in its direction. Intelligence and courage are its hallmarks and added to this is a gentle disposition. Like the Siamese, it demands affection and returns it in full measure, displaying particular devotion to its owner. Unlike the Siamese, however, it is not noted for vocal communication and its voice is soft, not raucous. Hardly surprising, therefore, that more and more people are finding the Abyssinian a charming, undemanding pet with an ideal temperament for the

show bench.

Another most attractive Foreign Short-haired breed, possessing features common to Siamese and Abyssinian cats, yet with a highly individual appearance and temperament, is the Burmese. The Brown Burmese is an established favourite and genuinely had its origin in Burma. It was from this country that the first female was imported into North America in 1930 by Dr Joseph C. Thompson of San Francisco. The cat was greatly admired and since a male of her own breed was not available she was mated with a Siamese male. The males from the resulting litter were then mated back to the mother, producing attractive, dark brown kittens. After breeding true for a number of generations, the Brown Burmese received official recognition in 1936 but it was not until after the Second World War, in 1947, that a British breeder introduced an American pair to Britain. The Brown Burmese received a breed number in 1952.

Burmese — Brown and Blue
Something of the original Siamese stock still shows through, although neither the slender body nor the wedge-shaped head are quite as long as those of the Siamese. The body is medium in size, neat and firm, with a slender neck. The legs should be long and slim and, as in the Siamese, the hind legs are slightly longer than the forelegs so that there is a gentle slope up from shoulders to hindquarters. Although the head is wedge-shaped, the top of the skull is slightly rounded and the features tend to be shorter and blunter, giving a rather softer general effect than the face of the Siamese. The ears, large at the base, are set fairly wide apart but again are not as prominent as those of the Siamese, being rounded at the tips. The long thin tail tapers to a point and a slight kink at the tip is permissible at shows. The eyes are almond shaped and the recommended colour is yellow or gold, but the majority have eyes of chartreuse-yellow (greenish-yellow). Burmese with blue eyes or with squints are inadmissible.

The coat, which should be glossy, short, fine in texture and lying close to the body, must be solid, rich, dark

Left The Burmese is a Foreign Short-hair. The face is somewhat rounder than that of the Siamese and the ears are set wide apart. The almond-shaped eyes should ideally be yellow.
Following pages left The Tabby Point Siamese is a very attractive cat, originally the result of an accidental mating of a Seal Pointed Siamese female and a Tabby male.
Above right A Tabby Point gets some outdoor exercise. In the United States the cat is known as the Lynx Point. Owners claim that it is the gentlest of all Siamese cats.
Below right A Blue Point Siamese.

seal-brown, shading to a slightly lighter hue on chest and belly. No white or tabby markings are allowed. Ears, mask and points should be a little darker than the colour of the back coat; but in kittens and young cats greater contrast is permitted between the coat colour, the mask and the points.

The Siamese features are even more noticeable in the delightful kittens. Born the colour of weak coffee, their coat grows gradually darker and faint points are soon visible. At about one year the true rich seal-brown colour is developed, although the chest and belly remain paler.

In 1955 a litter of Burmese kittens contained one with a lovely bluish-grey coat. Selective breeding in due course produced the Blue Burmese, this time recognized in Britain and Europe before being accepted in America. Body shape and coat texture are exactly as for the Brown Burmese but the colour is predominantly bluish-grey, darker on the back than on the underparts — a warm colour with a beautiful silvery sheen. Ears, mask and points should shade to silver-grey.

Breeders are continually experimenting with Burmese cats to produce new colour types and already an exciting new range is beginning to appear, including Cream, Red, Blue-Cream, Champagne, Lilac and Tortoiseshell.

Previous pages above left A Blue Burmese mother and kittens.
Below left Family of Tabby Point Siamese.
Right A Red Abyssinian. Each hair of the coat is ticked with bands of different colour but with no trace of black.
Above left This Chocolate Point Siamese and Irish Wolfhound are firm friends.
Far left The ground colour of the standard Abyssinian cat is russet-brown and the individual hairs are banded with dark brown or black.
Left The coat of this Blue Burmese kitten is bluish-grey with a silvery sheen.
Right The Blue Burmese is the newer of the two colour types but not the last word in selective breeding. Experiments to produce other colours are already under way.

Pretty as a Picture

The cat is a rewarding subject for the artist and the photographer. It has been said that it poses instinctively as if aware of its innate charm and beauty. The truth is, though, that the cat, whether in repose or in action, is naturally photogenic. The expressiveness of its face is the delight of the close-up specialist; and each of the many different breeds has its own special appeal and individuality.

Before the camera was invented many artists portrayed cats, often their own pets, although not necessarily as the central feature of their pictures. During the centuries when superstition was rife and cats were execrated as allies of the devil, few painters cared to depict them in a sympathetic role. There were, nevertheless, certain exceptions. Leonardo da Vinci, for example, applying the same careful observation and attention to detail that he brought to every subject that interested him, made some charming sketches of cats. Other artists found an ingenious way of lightening a religious theme and providing a refreshingly intimate touch to their work by including a domestic cat in the picture. One of the most delightful examples is the *Holy Family* by Federigo Baroccio, in which the smiling attention of the four human figures — Mary, Joseph, the infant Jesus and the child John the Baptist —

Artists through the ages have portrayed the cat in various guises. Here are three interesting and very different examples.
Above right *Detail from* The Holy Family *by Baroccio.*
Right *Richard Lindner's* Homage to a Cat.
Far right *Perronneau,* Girl with a Kitten.

is directed towards the cat in the lower left-hand corner of the canvas. In Ghirlandaio's *Last Supper*, on the other hand, the cat seated next to Judas is an incarnation of the devil; and the cats depicted in two of Tintoretto's religious paintings look equally malevolent.

By the eighteenth century the age of witchcraft was over and the cat was once more accepted on its own terms. Hogarth, depicting the uglier aspect of human nature, included a number of scrawny, emaciated cats in his engravings. In one illustration from the series entitled *The Four Stages of Cruelty* he showed one such unfortunate animal being suspended upside-down from a post and another being tossed from an attic window, attached to a pair of small balloons, evidently with a view to making it fly. But Hogarth made amends by showing a healthy cat in pleasanter domestic surroundings in his painting *The Graham Children*.

England and France were two of the countries where the virtues of cats seemed to be especially appreciated by writers and painters. In England Morland, Barlow and Stubbs all featured cats in their pictures. There is one, for example, in Stubbs's famous portrait of the racehorse Arabian Godolphin.

In France Watteau, Boucher and Fragonard all painted cats but only Watteau, judging from his sketches, really seems to have cared for the animal. There is more charm and realism in a portrait by a less familiar painter, Perronneau, entitled *Girl with a Kitten*. Delacroix and Géricault, normally associated with grander, wilder themes, both portrayed domestic cats with warmth and sympathy; and Manet, Renoir, Gauguin and Bonnard were among French painters of a later generation who found the cat worthy of their talents.

The Swiss artist Théophile Alexandre Steinlen depicted cats in less fashionable surroundings, prowling the streets and rooftops of Paris; and another Swiss, Gottfried Mind, confined his paintings to two kinds of animals — bears and cats.

The cat pictures of the English artist Louis Wain often descended to caricature but played an important part in popularizing cats, for they appeared everywhere — in books, magazines and newspapers and on postcards and calendars. Wain was drawing from first-hand experience for he was at one time a cat breeder and show judge.

Lens-eye view
Today the camera has replaced brush and paint. The popularity of the cat, both for its own sake and as a publicity aid, seems boundless, with Siamese and Persians the clear favourites. Beautiful cats and adorable kittens peer out from book jackets, magazine covers, calendars, cards and lids of chocolate boxes. On television they appear in advertisements not only for pet foods but also in more improbable contexts. This type of work is not for the ordinary cat. A great deal of patience and expertise is required, for the cat, given its self-willed temperament, is notoriously difficult to pose for a portrait; and not every model cat will adjust easily to the light, heat and bustle of a modern television studio. In this highly competitive field luck and 'star' quality are the keys to success.

Cat photography at its best is a random combination of skill, luck and patience. Not all subjects are this accommodating.
Left *Chinchilla kitten at a show.*
Right *Kitten through the looking glass.*

Rarities and Newcomers

A breed may be rare for one of several reasons. It may have existed for decades, even centuries, but having gradually waned in popularity will have lost favour with breeders, the result being that it is no longer seen in large numbers. Another breed may have lost its original body type or pure coat colour as a consequence of generations of random mating; and another may appear briefly — as a freak with features that breeders have no interest in perpetuating — and just as quickly vanish. Many colour types refuse to breed true so that the occasional specimen only appears as a result of experimental cross-breeding. Finally there are the genuinely new breeds, products of selective mating over several generations, perhaps still few in number but increasingly popular.

In the category of those breeds which are comparatively rare

Below Long-haired Tortoiseshell and White kitten.
Right A Long-haired Silver Tabby and her appealing kitten.
Following page left This fierce-looking cat is a Spotted Silver male.
Above right The true Manx cat or 'Rumpy' is completely tailless.
Below right Show standards permit the coat of a Manx cat to be any colour. The lack of a tail does not prevent the cat being as athletic as other breeds.

because of problems encountered in the genetic pattern, mention has already been made of the Tortoiseshells and Tortoiseshell and Whites, both in the Short-haired and Long-haired classes. In these breeds the rare males are invariably sterile. Equally difficult to breed because of the unpredictable mating pattern are the variously coloured Tabbies — Red, Silver, Brown and even Blue. Some of the self-coloured Persians, such as the Blue-Cream and the Solid Red, are also seen all too rarely because of breeding difficulties. Nor is it easy to produce a pedigree Long-haired Odd-Eyed White, with its pure white coat and differently coloured eyes, one deep blue, the other orange.

The tailless Manx

Nature plays strange tricks in the animal world and it was sheer accident that produced the Manx cat — easily identifiable from all other breeds by the fact that it lacks a tail. Although we now know that this must have come about as a consequence of genetic mutation we have no idea as to how, when and where it originally happened; but there is no shortage of legendary material to compensate for the absence of fact and to explain this shortcoming.

According to the oldest version, an impatient Noah, with an eye on the rising flood waters, slammed the door of the Ark on the cat, neatly slicing off its tail. Another story, trying to pinpoint the place of origin, tells how warriors defending the Isle of Man against Irish invaders, who wore plumes in their helmets, decided to decorate their own helmets in similar fashion. So they took to kill-

ing the local cats and using the bushy tails as battle emblems. One astute old female cat proceeded to have her next litter on a high mountain top, biting off the tails of her kittens and thus saving their lives. What is more, she passed on her secret to later generations, so that successive mothers continued to do the same, until eventually all Manx kittens were born without tails.

A less fanciful legend dates from the time of the Spanish Armada, when one of the galleons attempting to struggle home after the great naval defeat was wrecked off the coast of the Isle of Man and a number of tailless cats swam ashore from the sinking ship. There is no evidence, however, of this particular wreck and, furthermore, no proof that cats without tails ever lived in Spain. The original genetic mutation may have occurred on the Isle of Man, although it is interesting to note that tailless cats are today also found in Japan and Malaya. Be that as it may, the island claims the breed for its own, features it on the reverse side of its coins and has established a cattery to ensure that it does not die out.

The taillessness of the Manx cat is in fact a physical defect. At the end of the backbone, where the vertebrae of the tail normally begin, there is a distinct recess or hollow. The true, completely tailless Manx is known as a 'Rumpy' but occasionally a purebred Manx cat with a vestige of a tail will appear and this is called a 'Stumpy', which is not acceptable for showing. Unfortunately, breeding of true Manx cats is complicated by the fact that when Rumpies are mated together for several generations a lethal factor in the genetic pattern often emerges, killing the kittens either just before or just after birth. Although at one time breeders were unable to eliminate this mysterious factor it is now possible to minimize the risk by mating Rumpy males with Stumpy females.

The lack of a tail does not seem to handicap the Manx or prevent it keeping its balance when jumping from a height; but trouble may arise if other vertebrae of the spinal column are missing. In all other respects the cat is intelligent, affectionate and adaptable, easy to train (it will take quite happily to the lead) and particularly good with children.

In a good show specimen the taillessness is complete and there is a decided hollow at the end of the backbone, the rump ideally being as round as an orange. The hind legs are longer than the forelegs and this gives the cat a peculiar rabbit-like hopping gait. The head should be round and large, the nose longish but not too pointed or snipy, which is regarded as a fault. In fact the prominent cheeks tend to prevent this. The ears are fairly wide at the base, tapering to a point.

The coat of a Manx cat must be 'double', like that of a rabbit, with two layers that consist of a topcoat with soft, open fur and a thick, close undercoat. But the colour of the fur is immaterial. Recognized colours are the same as for standard Domestic Short-hairs, including White, Black, Red, Tortoiseshell and Bicoloured. Eye colour is not all that important and is only taken into account if all the other points are equal. Eyes should be large and round and ideally conform to the standard for the coat colour.

Cats with curly coats

Until quite recently all cats were distinguished by having long-haired or short-haired coats, the individual hairs of either type being straight. Now, however, there is a third type in which the coat is curly, each hair being waved. Cats with this unusual and very distinctive type of wavy coat are known as Rex-coated cats.

It was in 1950 on a farm in Cornwall that a litter of kittens was born to a Tortoiseshell mother and a father of unknown breed. One of the kittens had a peculiar curly coat and was recognized by an expert as being unique. When it grew to maturity it was mated back to the mother in an attempt to reproduce the mutant gene. The strange, short, silky coat appeared in half of the kittens in the ensuing litter. It was noticeable that the body hair of these kittens was much shorter than on normal Short-haired cats and that each hair was waved. Furthermore, no guard hairs were visible because they were shortened to just below the level of the topcoat; hence only the undercoat was in evidence. The whiskers and eyebrows were similarly wrinkled. The breed was given the name of Cornish Rex.

Some years later another curly-coated kitten appeared in Devon in a litter of Foreign-type cats. At first it was assumed that this kitten was similar to the Cornish Rex, but cross-matings proved unsuccessful for the resultant kittens all had the normal straight hair. It was concluded, therefore, that two different genes were involved. The Devon Rex, as it was named, had a much shorter, crisper coat as against that of the Cornish which was soft and warm to the touch. Subsequent selective breeding has lengthened the coat of the Devon Rex but it is not usually as thick as that of the Cornish Rex.

At around the same time a Rex-coated cat appeared in Germany but did not breed true. The two standard types, Cornish and Devon, have now been exported to the United States and other countries; and theoretically any other type, including Long-hairs, can be produced with the distinctive curly coat devoid of guard hairs. Strictly speaking, the term Rex refers to a coat type rather than a breed.

Standards for the Cornish Rex and Devon Rex call for a long, slender body, medium-sized, hard and muscular. The legs are long and fine with small, oval paws. The tail is long and whip-like, the neck slender. The profile varies slightly, that of the Cornish being straight and that of the Devon almost aquiline. In America Rex cats with coarse or guard hairs are disqualified. In Britain white mismarkings are faulted. As with Manx cats any coat colour or pattern is permissible. Apart from its unusual appearance, the Rex cat is healthy and undemanding — altogether an amenable, friendly pet.

Spotted cats

Most cats with patterned coats display a miscellany of stripes, bars and irregular blotches, sometimes interspersed with spots. It may seem surprising that more domestic cats have not emulated their wild cousins in acquiring a spotted coat. The truth is that although spotted household cats go back many centuries (the noble Catesby family, for example, has a spotted cat on its crest), they are exceedingly difficult to breed in such

a way as to conform to show stand-ards. The important thing is not so much the outline of the spots, which may be round, oblong or rosette-shaped, as their distribution. Each spot, whether large or small, has to be clear and distinct, not merging into another, and although the background colour is immaterial the spots must contrast with it in tone. Furthermore, the entire body must be spotted, the only permissible bars and stripes being on the face and head. Such a cat, seen at rest, often appears to be striped or barred and the individual spots only show to best advantage when it is moving. In kittens, too, the marks sometimes appear as solid lines of colour down the spine but tend to break up as the cats mature.

Standards for Spotted cats are as for all Domestic Short-hairs and a variety of interesting colour combinations are once more being bred, including handsome Reds, Blues, Browns, Silvers and Tabbies. Breeders hope that these cats will regain some of the popularity in shows that they evidently enjoyed in the early years of this century.

Siamese-type newcomers

A perfect example of a man-made breed is the Chestnut-Brown Foreign, originally known in Britain as the Havana. This latter name was dropped to avoid giving the impression that the breed originated in Cuba but in America the name has been retained.

The Chestnut-Brown has Siamese blood in its veins. A black female kitten born as a result of mismating between a Black Long-haired female and a Seal Pointed Siamese male was again mated to a Siamese. In her litter was an all-brown male kitten which became the progenitor of a new breed.

Recognized in 1958 and shown in the United States in the following year, the Chestnut-Brown's coat is short and glossy in a solid, warm mahogany or chestnut colour, not as deep as that of a Brown Burmese and without any markings or white spots. The kittens are born with their adult coat but sometimes show faint tabby 'ghost' markings that later disappear. The shape of the body differs too from that of the Burmese or Siamese,

being sinuous, finely boned and gracefully proportioned, never heavy. The wedge-shaped head should be set low on the neck and is longer than it is wide. The ears are set wider apart than in the Siamese and are pricked forward. The slanting eyes should be chartreuse-green. The breed, described in America as having a 'pixie' look, is rapidly gaining popularity.

The Foreign White, only recently recognized as a breed, is really a Siamese without points, first bred in Britain in 1962 from Siamese, British Whites and Havanas. The cat looks exactly like a Siamese in body shape — long and svelte with a wedge-shaped head, large, wide-based, pricked ears, vivid blue, almond-shaped eyes and a long, whip-like tail. But its coat is pure white without any shading at all on points and mask. As is common with all new breeds, a number of years were allowed to elapse to determine whether the Foreign White would breed true. It is interesting to note that this lovely cat, despite its white coat and blue eyes, possesses perfect hearing.

Similar to the Foreign White but actually a descendant of the Lilac Pointed Siamese is the Foreign Lilac, known in the United States as the Foreign Lavender. Although the breed has won partial recognition in America it has not yet been awarded a breed class in Britain. It is a self-coloured Siamese-type cat with the typical slender body and pointed head, its coat a faded lavender with no shading on points and mask. The slanting eyes are a brilliant apple-green. The Foreign Lilac is not an easy cat to breed for each parent must carry both blue and chocolate genes; but since it apparently breeds true to type and colour there is every chance that this attractive cat will eventually gain full recognition and start winning awards at shows.

Another genuine arrival from the East which has been recognized in the United States but not so far in Britain is the Korat. Whereas the background of the Siamese is shrouded in legend, with some doubt as to

A lovely Shell Cameo cat. There are four recognized colour types of this breed which is similar to the Chinchilla.

whether it even originated in the country whose name it bears, the Korat really does come from Thailand, where it is highly esteemed. The first male and female were exported to the United States in 1959 and since then breeding has been successful enough for the cats to be entered for shows.

The Korat is a medium-sized cat, well muscled and slightly more rounded than the Siamese. The legs are slender with dainty, oval feet. The head is small and the face heart-shaped, this effect being particularly accentuated in the male which has a small indentation between the wide-based, rounded ears. The large, prominent eyes are bright amber-green and the coat is a beautiful solid slate-blue, each hair being tipped with silver. The leather of the nose and pads is dark lavender blue.

Rare American breeds

Mutant genes can not only produce cats with curly coats, such as the Cornish Rex and Devon Rex, but also cats with virtually no hair at all. Such a cat was the Mexican Hairless,

a breed once found in America but now believed to be almost extinct. This cat was not completely bald, as its name might imply, for even the kittens were born with a few hairs which later dropped out and were replaced by a very short coat of downy fuzz. In general appearance it was midway between a cat and a rat, with large ears, a naked tail, a brownish back and pinkish underparts. In winter it would develop a ridge of fur along the spine. Although breeders had little difficulty in reproducing the responsible recessive gene, the cat was decidedly ugly and never won wide popularity, this being the main reason for its subsequent disappearance from the scene.

An American breed which has stayed the course for more than a century is the Maine Coon cat. Inhabitants of the New England state of Maine used to declare that the animal was a cross between a cat and a raccoon but this is quite impossible. Probably it was descended from Long-haired Tabbies which were allowed to run wild by the early

settlers. But since both the shape of the legs and the pattern of the coat show some resemblance to the raccoon, the original name has remained. The cat is powerfully built, the fur is long and thick (in a wide range of colours), the head is pointed and the eyes, though rounded, sometimes show a slight slant. The tail, unlike that of the typical Persian, is thicker, with longer hairs at the base than at the tip.

The American Cat Fancy also recognizes a number of other Long-haired cats that are seldom seen in Britain. The Shaded Silver, for example, is similar in appearance to the Chinchilla but the hairs of its coat are more heavily ticked. The undercoat is, therefore, grey whereas that of the

Below A Turkish Van mother and kittens — beautiful cats with long, silky coats.
Right The Devon Rex is one of two curly-coated breeds originating in England's west country.
Below right A Foreign White kitten. This recently recognized breed is a Siamese-type cat without points.

Chinchilla is white, producing an overall effect of pewter rather than silver. It is accepted as a separate breed on the Continent as well as in the United States, but not any longer in Britain.

The Masked Silver is also a Chinchilla-type cat and resembles the Shaded Silver except for the face which displays a dark mask, the paws being in a matching colour. The eyes of both these breeds may be emerald or blue-green.

Similar to the Chinchillas and Silvers, but with red ticking, are the beautiful Cameos. These have been successfully bred in the United States for more than twenty years but, although recognized there, are not yet accepted by the Cat Fancy in Britain. General standards are as for regular Persians and basically their coat colour is a combination of cream and red. The four recognized shades of Cameo are Shell, Shaded, Smoke and Tabby.

The Shell Cameo has a pale cream, almost white, undercoat; and the hair on the back, flanks, head and tail is delicately and lightly tipped with red. Face and legs may also be slightly ticked but the pale colour, without any ticking, appears on the chin, ear tufts, chest and belly. In the Shaded Cameo the ticking is heavier, producing a hot glow, but the red fades into the sides and turns ivory-white on the underparts. The Smoke Cameo has an even deeper colour — reddish-beige with a contrasting cream or white undercoat, red or deep beige points, and a mask with a white or pale cream neck ruff and ear tufts. No brown tinge or tabby markings are permitted in this breed; but well defined red or beige tabby markings break the otherwise even pale cream ground colour of the Tabby Cameo. In all four breeds the

Above left This stretching kitten is a Red Point Siamese with a Rex coat, offspring of a Siamese mother and a Rexhaired Tabby father.
Left The coat of the Korat kitten is slate-blue with a glistening sheen imparted by the silver-tipped hairs.
Right The Foreign Lilac or Foreign Lavender is another Siamese-type cat which is difficult to breed. In this litter only one kitten resembles its mother, the rest are Lilac Point Siamese.

Left A Manx father and his kitten. The high hindquarters of the cat give it a rabbity gait.
Below The Cornish Rex cat first appeared by accident when a pair of farmyard cats produced one kitten with a curly coat. It is now a registered breed and has been widely exported.

Right The Chestnut-Brown cat has Siamese blood, for the first specimen was the result of mismating between a Long-haired Black female and a Seal Point male.

Below A pedigree Red Tabby with correct, contrasted red ground colour and markings is not easy to breed.

Above left *An elegantly posed Red Colourpoint kitten.*
Left *Long-haired Tortoiseshell and White or Calico cat.*
Above right *A handsome Spotted Red cat.*
Right *A pair of Balinese kittens. Recognized only in the United States, this breed is the nearest yet to a true Long-haired Siamese.*

general effect, as in the Chinchillas and Silvers, should be brilliant and sparkling.

The Himalayan or Colourpoint has been mentioned in a previous chapter. It is a Persian cat with Siamese coloration, and in America the Red Point and the Frost Point are recognized in addition to the four other standard types. Similar to it, but only thus far recognized in France, is the Khmer.

Left The Maine Coon was once thought to be a cross between a cat and a raccoon. It is probably descended from stray Long-haired Tabbies.
Below Two Chestnut-Brown or Havana cats.

Still to gain universal acceptance, though recognized in America, is a genuine Long-haired Siamese known as the Balinese. This is a tall, aristocratic cat with a long, slender body, dainty legs, neck and tail, and small, oval paws. The face is typically wedge-shaped and the ears large, pricked and wide, but the eyes are large and round. In a really good specimen the fur should be at least two inches long. The Balinese exists in Seal, Blue, Chocolate and Lilac pointing.

The Peke-faced Persian, so called because its face resembles that of a Pekinese dog, with heavy jowls and large, prominent ears, is yet another breed only recognized in the United

States. Descended from Red and Red Tabby Long-hairs, this cat has a high forehead which bulges over the nose to create a sharp stop. The nose is very short, depressed and indented between the eyes and in profile is completely hidden by the full, round cheeks. A curious feature of the Peke-faced Persian's appearance is that it often seems to be crying. The reason is that wrinkled folds of skin under the eyes cause blockages of the tear ducts and lead to excessive watering of the eyes. This watering frequently stains the cat's long fur. The coat should be soft and fine, generously distributed over the whole body, including the shoulders. The ruff should be very large and

continue in a deep frill between the legs; the tail plume too should be very full. Classes are recognized for Solid Reds and Red Tabbies and no white markings are permissible.

Sacred cats and swimmers

Another cat with Siamese colouring is the French Birman, also known as the Sacred Cat of Burma. Like the Siamese this breed too has been accorded the privilege of having been traditionally worshipped in Buddhist temples. The famous legend concerning the Sacred Cat tells of a chief priest who lived, long before the coming of Buddha, in the mountains of Indo-China. His companion was a white cat called Sinh, which acted as his oracle. Together they would sit before the image of a golden goddess with sapphire eyes who presided over the transmigration of souls. One night, when the priests were gathered in the temple to pray to the goddess for protection against a foreign invasion, the old man suddenly died. His cat immediately jumped onto the throne of the goddess and rested against its dead master's head. The soul of the departed priest at once passed into the body of the cat, whose fur miraculously took on the golden hue of the statue, its yellow eyes turning to deep blue, its ears and paws to the colour of the earth. Only the tips of the paws remained white where they had touched the body of the dead priest.

The transformed cat then faced the outer door of the temple and the concentrated power of its gaze instilled the awe-struck priests with so much courage that they banded together to repel the invaders. Seven days later the cat, having refused food and water, also died, taking with it the soul of its master. The choice of a successor to the chief priest proved simple. The other hundred temple cats had by now also taken on the golden colour and blue eyes of the goddess and formed a circle round the youngest priest who was immediately elected to the vacant post.

Similar legends describe how the

This kitten is a Shaded Silver Persian, similar in appearance to the Chinchilla but with a grey, not white, undercoat. It is not yet recognized in Britain.

Above left An elegant Foreign White cat with typically pointed face, large ears, slanting eyes, oval paws and tapering tail. Although the eyes are blue this breed does not suffer from deafness.
Left The Birman cat, also known as the Sacred Cat of Burma, first won popularity in France. It is now bred in several colours both in Europe and America.
Right Despite their apparent difference these kittens come from the same Long-haired Tortoiseshell litter.

Left When these Turkish Van kittens grow they will probably take happily to water. Few other breeds are such accomplished swimmers.
Right The Tabby Cameo has dark tabby markings on a cream ground.

cat was kept in great luxury and worshipped by the priests in Burmese temples. Each priest believed that when he died his soul would enter the body of one of the temple cats. When the cat itself died the priest's soul would enter paradise.

Fanciful as these legends are, the Birman does indeed come from South-east Asia, the first pair being a gift to a British soldier from some Tibetan monks in 1919. The breed has been popular in France for some fifty years. Only quite recently, however, have its attractions become known in America and Britain. At first glance it looks like a Siamese with long hair but there are individual features that distinguish it both from the Balinese and the Colourpoint. The body is long and the legs stocky, with short paws. The head is round and slightly flattened on top, the cheeks full.

The fur is long, with a generous ruff, and silky in texture. The tail differs from that of the Colourpoint, being slightly longer and much bushier. The eyes are bright blue.

Seal and Blue varieties of the Birman are recognized in Britain but in America Chocolate and Lilac are also accepted for showing. The coat colour is beige but slightly more golden than that of the Siamese. Points are as in the Siamese but the feet are white.

The Turkish or Turkish Van cat is another breed which has been known in its homeland for hundreds of years but which has only recently been bred and exhibited abroad. It comes from the Lake Van region of south-eastern Turkey and is remarkable for its elegant, flowing, silky coat. The ground colour is white but it differs from that of the all-white Ankara cat

(still found in Turkey) by having rich auburn markings. The body is long and sturdy, the head wedge-shaped and longer than that of the normal Persian, the ears larger and more pointed, and the nose slightly sharper.

The light and dark auburn markings are most clearly defined on the head and tail, the latter being distinctly ringed in the two shades. The eyes are round, amber and pink-rimmed. These are standard markings but in Sweden Turkish cats have been bred with Red, Tortoiseshell and Tortoiseshell and White markings.

An interesting feature of the Turkish cat is that it not only swims but seems to take pleasure in the experience, whereas most other cats positively dislike water, or at best, merely tolerate it.

Left The Korat was originally imported from Thailand and has since been bred successfully in the United States.

Below left Only one kitten in this litter, certainly a female, takes after its Tortoiseshell and White mother.
Below Two Colourpoint kittens

Moods and Feelings

All animals in the wild communicate with others of their kind and with animals of other species by the best means available to them — by exhibiting bright colours, by displaying various offensive or defensive weapons in the form of claws, fangs, spines and so forth, by making use of special body movements or facial expressions, or by making sounds.

Those species that have been domesticated by man also manage to communicate expressively and vocally. Dogs and cats, in particular, succeed in conveying specific information concerning their own feelings and desires to their owners; the tones and dynamics of the sounds will indicate whether they are being playful, whether they are hungry or whether they are in pain.

Anyone who has ever owned a cat will readily attest to the amazingly wide repertoire of expressions and noises employed by their pet in order to make its feelings known. The cat's face alone can convey a variety of moods — annoyance, boredom, fear, pleasure or pain. Some cats have so much personality that it is almost possible to read in their facial expressions every passing thought and reaction. The pupils of the eyes will widen and then contract, the ears will be pricked and then be flattened. Normally, the cat holds the ears erect, alert for any nearby sound, however faint; and a lazy twitch of the ears will acknowledge a message received; but when the ears are

Left I wouldn't come any nearer if I were you.
Above right Go ahead, I'd just like to see you walk out on me!
Right Will you kindly sit down and allow me to finish!

flattened and held close to the head this is a danger signal and it is just as well to keep your distance.

The face may be contorted in various other ways. When the mouth is closed the expression, as often as not, is one of calm and tranquillity; but when the mouth is opened wide to display the teeth the effect can be either surprisingly funny or unexpectedly chilling. Cats definitely possess a sense of humour but not at their own expense. They are certainly not amused by being teased and hate to be laughed at. The 'laughing' expression that often flits over the face is accidental rather than deliberate — usually nothing more than a yawn to express fatigue or boredom. But the baring of the teeth may, on occasion, be a threatening gesture, comparable to the aggressive snarling of their larger cousins in the wild.

The tail too is often a reliable guide to a cat's mood. As a rule it is held firmly upright. When carried high above the back it conveys a sense of independence, perhaps indifference. When the tip is slightly turned over it expresses contentment and confidence; but when the tail is swished from side to side and fluffed up to twice its usual size it is a clear sign of discontent or positive anger. This warning signal is sometimes reinforced by arching the back, erecting a ridge of hairs along the spine, and spitting. Rubbing the body

against your leg is an obvious pledge of affection. The attentive owner will soon learn to recognize these and other subtle body and tail movements designed to convey information.

Where the cat scores over other domestic animals (including the dog, whose vocal equipment is virtually restricted to barks, growls and yelps) is in the enormous range of sounds it is capable of making. These sounds are, except during an all-male fight or when intended to convey a sexual message to another cat, moderate in pitch; but they include soft purring, gentle mewing, throaty **growling**, excited twittering, angry hissing, agonized wailing, exultant miaowing and much more besides.

The cat will use its voice to demand, cajole, bully or simply converse, leaving you in absolutely no doubt when it is hungry, cross or disapproving; and the soft purr of contentment is utterly individual to the species and quite unmistakable. It will use all the sounds in its repertory, according to the circumstances, but a mother will reserve her curious chortling, chirping noises for her kittens — a private language not designed for humans.

Left That's the best I've heard in years.
Below I hope you won't be offended if I tell you in confidence ...

On with the Show

In 1871 Mr Harrison Weir, an artist and ardent cat lover, organized the first official cat show at the Crystal Palace in London. Six years later he became the first President of the newly founded National Cat Club.

The Club, among its other functions, kept a register of pedigree cats in Britain, fixed standards for recognized breeds and issued a stud book in 1893. In 1908 the Club combined with a rival organization to form the Cat

Below *A pair of adorable Chinchilla kittens at a show. This breed is a long-established favourite.*
Right *Moment of triumph — a Champion Long-haired White is hoisted aloft.*

Fanciers' Association and in 1910 the Governing Council of the Cat Fancy was set up. This body encourages and promotes interest in pedigree breeding, keeps a national register of such cats, organizes and lays down the rules for shows and makes the Championship awards.

Various cat clubs both in Britain and abroad are affiliated to the Governing Council, whose work over the years has stimulated the establishment of similar organizations in other countries where pedigree cats are bred and exhibited. In North America the first show to be devoted exclusively to cats was held in New York's Madison Square Garden in 1895. The organizer of this event was an Englishman, James H. Hyde, who brought with him the schedules of the Crystal Palace shows. Public interest proved so great that a number of American cat clubs were formed in subsequent years, many of the finest cats being imported from Britain. Although it has not been practicable to have a single governing body, there are today in the United States many clubs that cater for all varieties, as well as larger associations fostering general interest in cats and setting standards for recognized breeds. The largest of these organizations is the American Cat Fanciers' Association.

Show procedures
Methods and procedures vary in different countries. In Britain there are three types of show. Exemption shows are fairly informal, though professional judges officiate, and these provide valuable experience for beginners. Sanction shows are virtually dress rehearsals for the Championship shows at which the finest specimens of each breed compete against one another for Championship certificates. The various cat clubs all over the country hold their own shows but the highlight of the year is the National Cat Club Show held at Olympia in London every December. At this and most other shows there is a special section for non-pedigree household cats in addition to the three principal classes — Long-haired, British Short-haired and Foreign Short-haired — for pedigree cats. The Household Pet section is divided into a number of classes which may include awards for the best Short-hairs and Long-hairs, kittens, cats with the most luxurious coat, the largest eyes, the most appealing expression and so forth. Neutered cats, provided they are registered, can also compete at Championship shows for Premier (but not for Championship) certificates. Non-registered neutered cats may also compete in the Household Pet classes.

At all shows held in Britain prize money is nominal. The coveted awards are the various trophies presented by the individual clubs for their own members and the certificates for the best male and female of each breed in open competition. In order to become a Grand Champion a Champion cat must compete against other Champions and win three Championship certificates, awarded by different judges of the breed at three separate shows.

In Britain a cat show is a one-day affair, usually held indoors during the autumn or winter, except in the case of kittens which are sometimes exhibited in the summer months. On the Continent cat shows sometimes last for two or three days, with members of the public admitted and quite a carnival atmosphere prevailing. Cat shows in Australia and New Zealand tend to be run as a rule on sedater British lines.

In the United States and Canada cat shows are held annually in many cities. The three principal classes for exhibition are Short-haired, Long-haired and All-breed; but here too there are special sections for kittens, neuters and household pets. Competition is for winners' ribbons which designate Championship points; and Champions with sufficient ribbons compete for Grand Championship status.

Although the points system that was originally devised by the Governing Council of the Cat Fancy has been adopted in principle by most exhibiting countries, there are certain other differences of detail, notably concerning the breeds that are recognized for show purposes and the standards laid down for these breeds. We have already mentioned in previous chapters a number of instances of cats that are recognized as separate breeds in some countries but not in others. Britain, for example currently has no Shaded Silvers, Cameos, Peke-faced Persians, Maine Coons and Korats on its lists — all of these being breeds that are regularly seen on show benches in America. Even when a breed is recognized on both sides of the Atlantic there may be slight variations in the stipulated standards and points allocation.

There is a significant difference too in the actual judging procedure. In Britain, parts of the Commonwealth and many European countries, the owner is normally required to leave the hall while judging is in progress. Each cat is removed from its pen and placed on a table by a steward for inspection by a judge. The owner is not permitted to intervene once the show is under way unless especially requested to do so by the show manager as, for example, in case of illness. The judge makes his decision privately and results are not announced until the end of the show. In America the system is quite different and there are variations too from one state to another. Usually the judge is seated at a long table in view of exhibitors and spectators alike. As the competitors' names are announced breeders or owners carry their cats to the table and are then permitted to watch the judging. The judge will often discuss the reasons for his findings with the exhibitor.

Exacting standards
The judges make their awards by reference to the standards laid down for particular breeds. We have alluded to these standards in discussing various breeds in previous chapters. Points are awarded to the total of 100, scaled differently for each breed but broadly devoted to such essentials as body type, coat colour, eye colour

Right American Seal Point Siamese Champion, Black Bart.
Following pages left
This Long-haired Brown Tabby has a white chin and cannot expect to win an award for pedigree cats.
Below left A Long-haired Blue and White cat, evidently in excellent condition for the show.
Right The emerald eyes of this pedigree Chinchilla contrast beautifully with the sparkling silver coat.

and condition. In the majority of Long-haired varieties the colour and texture of the coat are of paramount importance. Between 45 and 65 points may be awarded under the 'colour' and 'coat' headings, the balance being given in varying proportions for the shape of the body, the head, the eyes and the tail. In the case of Short-haired cats 50 points are awarded for eye colour and coat colour or markings; the other 50 points are for body type, coat and condition.

The scale of marking for Foreign breeds is more variable, according to individual peculiarities. Thus in the case of Siamese varieties there are 50 points for type and shape (of which 15 are for head, 15 for body and 5 each for ears, eyes, legs and paws, and tail); 35 for colour (15 for the eyes, 10 each for points and body colour); 10 for coat texture and 5 for condition. The Abyssinian is awarded up to 30 points for body colour and up to 20 for ticking.

As for the Manx cat, colour is relatively unimportant, meriting no more than 5 points; but no less than 65 points are given for such structural features as taillessness, height of hindquarters, shortness of back, roundness of rump and depth of flank.

Entry regulations
If you are the owner of a pedigree cat (by definition a cat whose ancestors are known for at least three generations) which you intend to enter for a show in Britain, you must first register it with the Governing Council of the Cat Fancy. No registered cat may be entered for an unlicensed show without the permission of the Council. Pedigree neutered cats also have to be

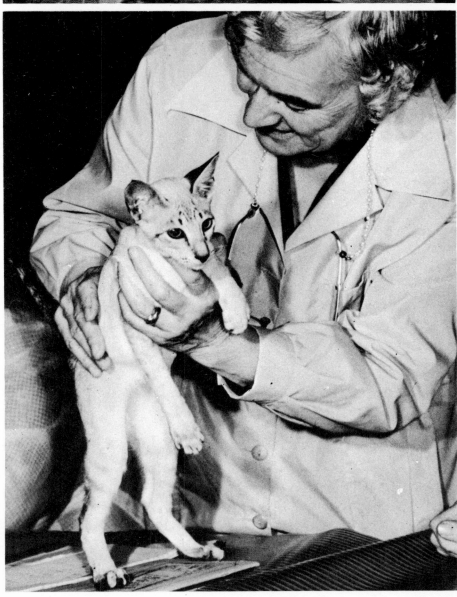

Above left A Birman cat and her kitten. *The points are dark brown, as in the Seal Point Siamese, but the paws are white.*
Left |*This Abyssinian crossed with a Silver Tabby could only be exhibited in the 'Any other variety' section.*
Above right An illustration from the Book of the Cat *by the famous fancier Frances Simpson, showing her judging at the Richmond Show of 1901.*
Right A judge examines a Tabby Point Siamese.

registered. Non-pedigree cats, including neuters, do not have to be registered and may be entered for competition in their appropriate classes.

Single kittens are not normally accepted for showing until they are three months old (four months in the case of Siamese and Burmese kittens). Only at a few shows held during the summer are eight-week-old kittens permitted. In some shows three or more kittens from the same litter — all aged between ten and twelve weeks — may be entered. Officially a kitten becomes a cat at the age of nine months.

A copy of rules for showing, issued by the Governing Council of the Cat Fancy, is sent out with entry forms and it is important to study these very carefully because any error or omission could lead to disqualification. Full information will also be provided regarding classes, judges and prizes.

Details to be filled in on the entry form must correspond with those on the cat's registration form. The name of the cat will often bear a breeder's prefix by which the cattery can be identified, this being a guarantee of quality in that it demonstrates the breeder's confidence in his cats. The completed entry form, together with the appropriate fee (which depends on the number of classes for which the cat is entered) should be sent to the show manager in good time. The closing date for entry is usually six weeks prior to the show. Accompanying the acknowledgment of the entry form will be a numbered tally which must be affixed by tape or ribbon around the cat's neck on the day of the show.

The strictest precautions are taken at all cat shows to prevent the risk of infection, which is likely to spread rapidly in a crowded hall. It is compulsory for all kittens to have a certificate of inoculation against feline infectious enteritis, and it is advisable for any cat to pay a visit in advance to the local vet in order to make quite sure that it is fit for showing. No cat will, in any event, be admitted to the show hall on the day without being vetted-in. The veterinary surgeon on duty will examine each entrant for any signs of ill health, searching particularly for parasites in the fur and ears. Should he not be satisfied, the cat will be sent home or isolated. If all is well, it is admitted to the hall to be placed in the pen bearing its tally number.

Pre-show care

Although a show cat has no special food requirements, apart from a sensibly balanced and well varied menu, extra care must be taken to make sure that its coat is in tip-top condition. Special grooming should, therefore, commence at least one month before the big day. Long-haired cats need a great deal of pre-show preparation. They must be thoroughly brushed, combed and, depending on colour, powdered once if not twice daily. Short-haired breeds benefit from daily hand grooming so that the coat always lies completely flat.

White cats in particular must be kept very clean so as to prevent the coat becoming dingy or the tail turning yellowish. If sufficient care is taken over grooming it may only be necessary to apply talcum powder but sometimes an overnight bath may be required, care being taken to dry thoroughly. Powder should not be applied to cats with light-coloured coats, but coats of any colour may be dusted occasionally with bran which must, of course, be completely brushed and combed out afterwards. Dark-coated cats may be wiped over, after grooming, with a little eau-de-cologne, and Short-haired varieties given a concluding polish with a chamois leather or piece of silk. Finishing touches to grooming can be given on the morning of the show but powder should not be applied because the cat risks disqualification if any flecks are left in the coat and it is forbidden for an owner to brush them out in the hall.

It is absolutely essential to pay the closest attention to the extremities and the eyes and ears. The coat must be free of fleas and any sign of worm infestation is not tolerated. If, on the morning of the show, the cat is sneezing, has runny eyes or shows any other sign of being off-colour, swallow your disappointment bravely but do not on any account take it along to the hall.

It is inadvisable to exhibit a female which is still nursing, even if the kittens are aged eight to ten weeks. There will be a tendency for the milk glands to swell as the day goes on and this must inevitably lose points as well as causing distress to the cat.

Having brought your cat into peak condition for the occasion, you will have to decide on the best way of getting it to the show. Obviously this will depend on the distance involved and the method of transport available. If you own a cat which seems untroubled by long journeys in its basket or box, there will be no great problem. Some cats, however, object to be confined for any length of time and prefer travelling loose in a car or, even better, accept a lead. The important thing is that the cat should be mentally relaxed as well as physically fit when it reaches its destination.

Even if all goes well prior to the show, there is no guarantee that your cat will behave when judging actually starts. It is worth remembering that adult cats directly involved in breeding do not, as a rule, make good show cats. Stud cats may be disturbed, for example, by calling queens in the vicinity. An experienced fancier will know by consulting a diary which days are unsuitable for showing, depending on whether the cat is male or female. In other circumstances it may be a matter of keeping fingers crossed. The most even-tempered of cats may react unpredictably to show conditions, especially if this is its first appearance in public. It may be upset by the whole unfamiliar atmosphere, the bright lights, the presence of other cats, or perhaps being handled by strangers. In the academic world many a gifted student has been let down at the last moment by examination nerves and the same may happen to your cat at the show. Giving the cat a sedative in an effort to calm it down is strictly prohibited. All an owner can do is to take into account all foreseeable contingencies and hope for the best. In fact the majority of cats seem to revel in the atmosphere of the show and enjoy all the special fuss and attention.

In Britain the procedures for the various Championship shows follow a similar pattern. After the cat has

Champion Darling Dream Angus, Red Point Siamese.

186

been passed fit by the veterinary surgeon the owner is required to place it in the appropriately numbered pen in the show hall. A sanitary tray is provided and the floor of the pen, which will already have been disinfected, may then be covered with a plain white blanket, under which a hot water bottle can be placed, if desired. Any more elaborate type of furnishing, including coloured blankets, is prohibited and may lead to disqualification. The cat should not be given food prior to the judging and a final grooming session (but no powdering) is permitted at this stage. The exhibitor is usually required to leave the hall immediately the show manager opens the proceedings, but at the National Show in Olympia exhibitors and spectators are allowed to be present.

Win or lose

Each class has its own judge and steward whose services are given voluntarily. During the judging every precaution is taken to avoid spreading infection in the hall and all judges and stewards wash their hands in disinfectant before handling any cat. Each cat in turn is removed from its pen by a steward, placed on a table, examined by a judge and then returned to the pen. Ideally it should be relaxed and stand quietly while being handled. No word is spoken as the judge goes about his work and complete anonymity is assured by the fact that there is no other identification than the tally number around the neck of each cat.

When judging of each class is completed, the awards are announced on a board and later the individual award cards are posted on the pens of the fortunate winners. Owners of winners and losers alike are then permitted to feed their cats. The judges are available to discuss with disappointed exhibitors the reasons for points having been deducted — criticism which is often helpful for future occasions. is often helpful

The climax of a British cat show is the selection of the Best in Show, for which coveted award the winners from various classes compete openly with one another.

A whole day spent in the show hall is likely to be an exhausting experience for any cat. Since the majority of these shows are held in the autumn or winter the chances are that the cat will also be cold when you get it home. Special attention is therefore advisable at the end of the day. The cat should be given a tasty meal (a little brandy or whisky in warm milk is favoured by some breeders) and then rubbed gently all over with a mild disinfectant, special care being given to the paws, the corners of the eyes, mouth and ears. It should then be tucked up warmly and left to sleep. As an extra precaution against possible infection picked up at the show the cat should be kept well away from other cats and kittens for a few days.

Below A pair of award-winning Short-haired Spotted Tabbies from the Brynbuboo Cattery.
Right Champion Archsue Ginbunny, Long-haired Blue-Cream.

Index

Acknowledgments

The publishers would like to thank the following individuals and organizations for their kind permission to reproduce the pictures in this book:-

AGIP 174
Associated Freelance Artists Ltd/G. Kinns 10
Victor Baldwin 96 (top), 152, 163 (bottom), 172 (top), 181
Barnaby's Picture Library 70 (top right), 74, 88-9, 98, 112, 175 (bottom)
Bavaria Verlag 159
Bavaria Verlag/W. Lüthy 35 (bottom), 139
Sdeuard Bisserôt 22 (bottom), 69 (top right), 94 (bottom), 101 (bottom), 102 (top), 107 (top), 126 (top), 128 (top), 140 (bottom left), 162 (bottom), 182 (bottom), 184 (bottom)
Camera Press 14 (bottom), 16 (bottom), 46 (top), 172 (bottom)
J. Allan Cash 44 (bottom)
Bruce Coleman Ltd 6, 7, 125 (bottom)
Bruce Coleman Ltd/Jane Burton 42; Bruce Coleman/J. Pearson 15

Colour Library International 105 (bottom), 150-1
Anne Cumbers 22 (top), 33 (bottom), 37 (top), 41, 44 (top) 49 (top), 85, 90, 94 (top), 96 (bottom), 97 (top), 100 (top), 120, 131 (bottom), 138, 155, 156, 157 (bottom), 158 (bottom), 163 (top), 166-7, 168, 184 (top), 187, 188, 189
Dr Brian Eustace 185 (top)
FPG Inc. New York 102 (bottom), 164, 182 (top), 183
Will Green 23 (bottom), 161 (top)
Sonia Halliday 23 (centre), 170
Michael Holford 13
Louise Hughes 113
Keystone Press Agency 69 (top left), 95 (top left)
Mansell Collection 8 (top), 9
Mary Evans Picture Library 8 (bottom)
Jane Miller 60 (bottom), 70 (bottom), 72 (top), 81 (bottom)
John Moss 35 (top left), 36 (top), 115 (top)
National Gallery 19, 142 (top) 143
Natural History Photographic Agency 49 (bottom), 122, 129 (top) 131 (top)
Pictorial Press 20, 29, 30, 52 (bottom), 62, 65 (top), 68, 69 (bottom), 129 (bottom), 147, 162 (top), 175 (top), 177
Politikens Press Foto 80

Popperfoto 53 (bottom)
Radio Times Hulton Picture Library 1█ (bottom)
Spectrum Colour Library 12, 14 (to█ left), 16 (top), 34, 35 (top right), 4█ 48, 51, 52 (top), 53 (top), 54, 55, 56, ▌ (top), 61, 65 (bottom), 66, 73 (bo█ tom), 75, 78, 83, 84, 86, 92 (bottom), ▌ (bottom), 105 (top), 111, 115 (bo█ tom), 116, 121, 124, 148, 169, 173, 17█ 178, 179, 185 (bottom), end papers
Tony Stone Associates 26 (top), 59, ▌ (top left), 101 (top right)
Syndication International 31, 32, 37 (bo█ tom), 82 (top left), 117 (top), 118, 1█
Tate Gallery 142 (bottom)
Sally Anne Thompson 21, 23 (top), 24– 26 (bottom), 27, 28, 33 (top), 36 (bo█ tom), 38, 46 (bottom), 57, 58, 71, ▌ (bottom), 73 (top), 76, 81 (top), 82 (to█ right), 82 (bottom), 87, 92 (top), 93, ▌ (right), 95 (bottom), 100 (bottom), 1█ (top left), 103, 104, 106, 107 (bottom█ 108, 125 (top), 126 (bottom), 127, 12█ (bottom), 132-3, 134, 136, 137, 1▌ (top), 140 (bottom right), 141, 14█ 145, 146, 149, 157 (top), 158 (top), 16█ 161 (bottom), 165, 171
ZEFA/Gary C. Lewis 45

First published 1975 by Cathay Books
ISBN 0 904644 01 4
© 1975 Cathay Books
Printed in Czechoslovakia by PZ, Bratislava